The NVivo Qualitative Project Book

Patricia Bazeley and Lyn Richards

SAGE Publications
London • Thousand Oaks • New Delhi

First published 2000

Reprinted 2002

NVivo is a trademark of QSR International Pty Ltd.

SAGE Publications Ltd
6 Bonhill Street
London EC2A 4PU

SAGE Publications Inc
2455 Teller Road
Thousand Oaks, California 91320

SAGE Publications India Pvt Ltd
32, M-Block Market
Greater Kailash - I
New Delhi 110 048

British Library Cataloguing in Publication data

A catalogue record for this book is available from the British Library.

ISBN 0 7619 6999 3
ISBN 0 7619 7000 2 pbk

Library of Congress catalog card number available

Printed in Great Britain by The Alden Press, Oxford

The NVivo Qualitative Project Book

Contents

Preface

Qualitative computing has entered the mainstream. Tools provided by computer software to assist qualitative analysis have become acceptable, even assumed, just as it is assumed that one will use a word processor for writing, or a statistics program for quantitative analysis. With the new-generation qualitative software, NVivo, it is possible to manage, access and analyze qualitative data and to keep a perspective on all of the data, without losing its richness or the closeness to data that is critical for qualitative research.

A researcher approaching new software can feel overwhelmed by its apparent complexity. Many find manuals hard to use. They must offer detail when often only a simple explanation will suffice. They must deal with software functions in logical order, whilst the user often wishes to deal with issues as they are met on the path through a project. Thus, the manual seems remote from what is going on for the researcher who is embroiled in a particular topic and submerged in the data they are generating.

In this book we set out to introduce software tools as they are needed, placing them in context. By taking the researcher through their own project, step-by-step, in NVivo, we offer a different way of learning software, one which does not merely summarize functions but shows how the software helps researchers bring data "alive".

Like qualitative research, the task of writing this book demanded efficiency, creativity and boundless energy. We gratefully acknowledge contributions in each of these areas from many colleagues. The book's design was by Kirstie Taylor. Ted Barrington was reader, constructive critic and patient helper through the final stages. Alan Purdom created the artwork for the cover and title pages. The NVivo team at QSR prepared the CD that accompanies the book. And finally, our thanks to Tom Richards, chief architect of NVivo, on behalf of all those whose research, like ours, has benefited from his design.

Introduction: The book and the software

Researchers learning research software have a choice. Some prefer to know all the tools offered by the software and how they work before using them. But many learn better by employing the tools as they need them. Qualitative software is often best learned that way, since qualitative projects normally unfold; as more data are discovered or created, more ideas are formed, more hunches and theories constructed and tested, and more inquiries built on those first ideas. Doing qualitative research with software does not require a full knowledge of all the tools at once. So long as you know that you will not create future problems, or limit future choices, you can get on with a project and get to know the software as you go.

About this book

This book takes you through the basic steps for using a software package, QSR NVivo, with real data in a real project. You can work through your own project, or you can work with the data provided and share Pat Bazeley's processes of discovery in the Researchers project.

This is an entirely new approach. As teachers of research and research software, we have become aware of the need for a book for those who prefer to learn by doing. It is not an alternative to the manuals that accompany the full software, or the online Help and Glossary that are on both the full software and the CD-ROM in the back of the book. But it gives sufficiently detailed step-by-step instructions for a reader to set up and use a project without consulting those sources. You can use the Project Book without looking at the manuals or Help, rather as you get to know a new vehicle as you take it on a test drive, without reading the car's manual. If you go on to use the full software in your own project (or own the car), you should of course use the manuals to find all the options and processes available.

Before you test drive a particular vehicle, however, it is important to know how to drive! This book is not a text on qualitative research. It can be used (like the vehicle) by someone without a license, but at some risk. It will be more helpful to those who know what they are trying to do, who have done some reading and thinking about qualitative work, about the sort of data expected, and the sorts of analyses sought. Qualitative research involves methodological choices; there are very many different ways of doing it, and they require different sorts of data and different research strategies. This book can't help with those choices, though it does indicate tools available for different strategies. If you are meeting qualitative research for the first time, it is very advisable to do a course or to read about qualitative methods before starting your own real project. There are many websites offering useful references: the QSR websites, www.qsr.com.au and mirror sites, have basic readings and links to other sites.

In this book we have avoided commitment to one methodology. It is quite usual, but arguably not desirable, for researchers to meet and handle data pragmatically, reaching for tools as they seem needed. We take this pragmatic approach here, in order to show as wide a range of software tools as possible, but we do not recommend it for real projects. For most qualitative research it is important to specify a research approach, and seek a fit of question with approach to data-making and analysis.

About NVivo

What's new in this book is that it approaches software learning without requiring that you know all (or even much) about the software before you use it. So this section is brief. If you wish to have a full description of the software before starting learning it, go to the online Help and other documentation mentioned below.

Since this book tells the story of a project, its outline offers a starting picture of the toolkit in the software. NVivo is designed to approach qualitative analysis as researchers do. A project may start simply with a question or a purpose. NVivo will store those first ideas in rich text documents, and let you edit them as they change, and link what you write to other files as you go. These first ideas can be explored in a visual model. Follow these steps through Part 1 to get your project under way.

From this tentative beginning, researchers usually generate some first concepts, ideas or categories. NVivo will store these at nodes that can be explored, organized or changed. An early step may be to code the relevant parts of documents. In NVivo you can code in many ways as you read or edit. You can browse all the data coded at a node, reviewing the data, returning to the context, or rethinking the idea. Part 2 will introduce these steps.

Researchers may create data documents and edit them during a project (e.g. diaries, field notes) or import documents already typed up (interviews, focus groups, etc.). Documents can be edited or imported into the NVivo project in rich text format. Data outside the project can be represented in editable, codeable proxy documents. Most qualitative projects also involve some information about cases, sites or people, and researchers need this to use when questions are asked about the data. (Did only women express this concern?) NVivo stores such information in attributes of documents or nodes. Observations and reflections are recorded and ideas captured in memos about the documents or annotations in them. We arrive at this point at the end of Part 3.

Whilst working with data, the researcher normally does many things simultaneously. Interpreting a document and storing the ideas that emerge from it requires annotating, memoing, coding and reflecting about coding. Part 4 explores the many ways of linking, coding and reflecting on data. Coding now will become more systematic and be combined with reviewing and reporting on coding and using the ability to "code-on" to new categories. New insights are stored in a node's links and memos, and by reporting and modeling what has been found.

A project rapidly grows complex bodies of data and ideas about it. Part 5 provides guidance on shaping the data and ideas, using Trees for organizing nodes and Sets for organizing either documents or nodes. Categories for coding can be shaped using searches, and in this Part we introduce the integrated search tool for asking questions of coding, text or attributes and pointing the search exactly where you want your question asked. NVivo combines these options in a Search Tool that walks you into a search operation allowing you to specify the scope of the search and what you want to do with the result. Part 5 ends with a brief discussion of shaping of data from particular cases (people, sites etc.), by coding at a case node. Information about that case can be stored in node attributes.

What of the goal of making theory from the data? Tools that assist in theory emergence are introduced in Part 6. Clarification of concepts is done in many ways, working with text coded at a node, naming and describing it. The processes of building a web of ideas can involve linking to memos or text coded at a node, or to particular extracts of data. Category development can be done by focusing using searches, combining and reviewing nodes and modeling, with layers representing the growing ideas.

At this stage, the researcher may need to start ordering ideas in a more careful index system, so NVivo allows management of nodes in logical trees. Nodes are cut, copied, merged as the researcher gets a stronger feeling for what is going on in the data. Part 7 discusses the uses of node trees, and ways of sorting nodes into catalogues for easy access and review. And it offers ways of tightening and strengthening the project by managing nodes.

As researchers become more confident, they can use ways of moving faster, for example by handling the clerical tasks of import of documents, automating of coding and import of attributes. Part 8 shows how to do these tasks, suggests ways to speed up coding, then shows how to use these features to ask questions and seek patterns. Searching now becomes more subtle, specifying exactly the question to be asked and the scope of the search—where it will be asked. Searching usually becomes more intense and more complex as the data builds up. Part 9 discusses these strategies for managing data in case studies and ways of undertaking within case and across case analyses.

Part 9 is about getting there—wherever that required arrival point may be for your project. Almost all researchers have a goal of synthesis or adequacy of explanation, and NVivo's tools can help reach that goal. They include ways of assessing concepts, reviewing the performance of nodes and the node system, seeking and exploring associations and relationships, finding and validating patterns and above all, since this is usually the end point of qualitative research, returning to the data, for detailed understanding, insight, surprise and arrival.

An Appendix adds further detail for those who want it—on things you will find useful to know about Windows and Word, and on preparation of data for efficient processing in NVivo.

How can NVivo be used with this book?

You can follow the steps in this book using the demonstration software on the CD-ROM in the back, or using your own full software. With either the demonstration software or the full software, you can use either the project data provided (the Researchers project), or your own data. The Researchers project is introduced in Part 1: it contains real interviews and focus group transcripts from a real study about becoming and being a researcher.

If you have the full software, you can work on your project (or the Researchers project), take a break, and return to it. As you work through the book, your project will develop and mature.

If you use the demonstration software, changes to your project will not be saved. The steps in the book can be followed in several stages using the demonstration software with the Researchers project, since this project is provided on the CD at six different stages of development. You could use the demonstration software to follow the steps on your own project if you wish, but each time you close NVivo, the project will be lost. We recommend that if you do not have the full software you use the Researchers project so that you can progress through to the later stages of a project.

If you are a teacher, wishing to use this book whilst teaching with your own data in a class setting, you can use the full software to create and save projects with your data, and provide these as demonstration projects for students who do not have the full software to use alongside this book. If you need further advice to do this, email help@qsr.com.au.

What other help is there?

NVivo is very well documented, both on the computer and in written materials.

If you wish to supplement the information in this book on any question, go first to the online Help. Call Help with the **F1** key from any dialogue where you might like to know more about the options. Use the **Glossary** for a definition of any term used in the software.

Two books accompany the full software, a *Reference Guide* and a methods book, *Using NVivo in Qualitative Research*. If you do not have the full software, *Using NVivo* (by Lyn Richards, Sage Publications, London, 1999) can be purchased separately through your regular bookstore. On the QSR website you will find free teaching materials and introductory summaries as well as answers to Frequently Asked Questions.

If you go on to use the software, you will find there are many researchers around the world who help others to use it and who discuss research strategies on a very active QSR-Forum. The authors of this book are two of them. To join these conversations, or to get news about classes, training workshops, conferences and other events, or for contact with consultants who will help with your particular research needs, go to the QSR website (www.qsr.com.au), or email help@qsr.com.au.

Part 1: Making a start

The hardest part of a qualitative project can be to get started. This section and the software are designed to overcome that starting block.

The NVivo software is designed to make creating a project a minor task, and one that does not need to be delayed until you have some "real" data. Indeed, the easiest way to create data documents is to do it in the NVivo project. So we start there. A project in NVivo does not require any firm decisions or prior shaping. Make it, name it, and get on with the job.

Where to start?

Qualitative projects often start without a clear theory, a specific hypothesis or a firm research goal. If you *are* starting with those, you may already know what you are looking for, where to look and what you can expect to find. But whatever the qualitative method, projects more usually begin with a problem, a question or a puzzle and a sense that a lot more needs to be known before the researcher can start constructing theory, let alone make claims for it. By keeping questions open, we allow ourselves to be informed by the data, redirected, surprised. This requires holding on to rich data in context, with the option to return, revisit, rethink and reinterpret data as we get a firmer sense of what is going on.

This means the researcher approaching a project often has no clear starting line, no clearly marked track to follow and imperfect knowledge of the route or the endpoint. In such a situation it is hard to take the first step. And when it is taken, the early data can be daunting, since qualitative approaches create complex data that can't be tidied without risk of losing something you don't yet know is important.

There are many ways of putting off an "official" start. Rethink the topic, rewrite the proposal, redo the preliminary literature review. All of these are proper processes in qualitative research, but they are wasted if they are not treated as *part of the research*. Explorations of the topic, the proposal, the literature, are data. The project is underway once these are happening. From the beginning, then, we need ways of storing and exploring, reworking and revising those early thoughts and rethinks, tentative ideas, insights, despairing memos, or discoveries in unrelated literature. From this oddly assorted treasure trove of early materials, we build a project up, as a bower bird builds a nest.

Installing and calling NVivo

To use the software, you first have to install it on your computer and then "call" or "run" it. The installer built into the NVivo CD takes you through the few decisions necessary.

Whilst you are working in your project, you must have NVivo running. Other applications may be open on the computer at the same time (but check the computer has enough memory to run them adequately).

Installing NVivo

D.I.Y.

- If NVivo is not installed on your machine, insert in your CD drive the CD from the back of this book. An install wizard will take you through the few steps to install the software.

- If you have your own software but plan to use the Researchers project, you will then need to use the CD installer to install the relevant sample project files in your QSR Projects folder. After installation the CD can be removed.

- When it is installed, QSR NVivo will appear under Programs on the Start menu in Windows. To run it, as with any other application, simply select Programs, and then NVivo, from that menu.

Starting a project

This is possibly the simplest task in this book. When you call NVivo, a Launch Pad appears on the screen, offering options to create a new project, open a project or run a tutorial.

Projects can be created in typical or custom format. Custom format is for researchers who need to password protect their project, or to locate it somewhere other than the default QSR Projects folder.

Create a project

D.I.Y.

- From the Launch Pad, choose to Create a Project.

- The New Project Wizard offers a choice of a Typical or Custom project. Leave Typical selected (unless there are special circumstances which require a custom setup), and press Next.

- Give the project a Name and a Description. These can be changed later. (If you are using the data provided, call it Researchers and describe it as a project about becoming and being a researcher.) Click Next.

- Check the details about your project setup. Note that NVivo has placed your project in the QSR Projects folder, on your C drive. Click Finish.

You have a project!

First steps

Remember the feeling at school when you got a new exercise book, and tentatively made your first marks on it? You didn't want to spoil it, so you began with extra care and many promises to yourself about how well you were going to work in this new book.

A new project in NVivo requires less care. Any document can be edited, and any thinking about data can be revised or deleted. So the best advice is to start as soon as there is something to start with, and drop into the project anything that might be worth keeping. It can be discarded later if you decide it is not precious.

Recording your initial thoughts

Where to begin? You may have reviewed some literature, written a policy document, interviewed someone, or run a focus group. Later, these can be directly imported (see Part 3). But for now, for most projects, some thinking about what you're asking is the best place to begin. Start with a new blank document in NVivo where you can progressively record your thinking about this project.

Using the NVivo editor to create a new document

D.I.Y.

- From the Project Pad, choose to Make a Project Document. The New Document Wizard will open.

- Click the final option—to Make a new blank document, ready for use in the NVivo editor.

- Name the document, for example, "Project Journal."

- In the description slot, type a description that is useful, for example, "Record of my developing ideas about [topic]."

A new document is created. NVivo opens the blank document on screen in a Document Browser. The Browser offers a wide range of tools for editing, changing and coding the document.

Editing in the Document Browser

Just start typing as though in a word processor, and a first document is happening. Your record of ideas about the project can grow as you wish, and will provide a valuable history of the project. You can close it at any stage, reopen it when some more ideas occur and keep typing.

The NVivo Document Browser contains a rich text editor with familiar Edit menu items (Cut, Copy, Paste, Find, Replace). Font, colour, styles, and other formatting icons on the toolbar can be used to direct attention or add emphasis.

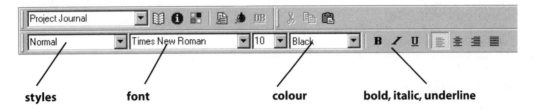

- Start by writing about the project's goals, for example
  - why you are doing it
  - what you think it's about
  - what are the questions you're interested in, and where those came from
  - what you expect to find, and the basis for that.

Feel free to edit the text you have written.

- Now go back to the top and type in a heading for this entry. Add the date by selecting Insert Date & Time from the Edit menu.

You can now use all the features of rich text to clarify your document, and to make it more meaningful and useful.

- With your cursor in your heading, select Heading 1 from the Styles slot in the formatting toolbar. The text for the whole heading will change to Arial 14-point bold type.

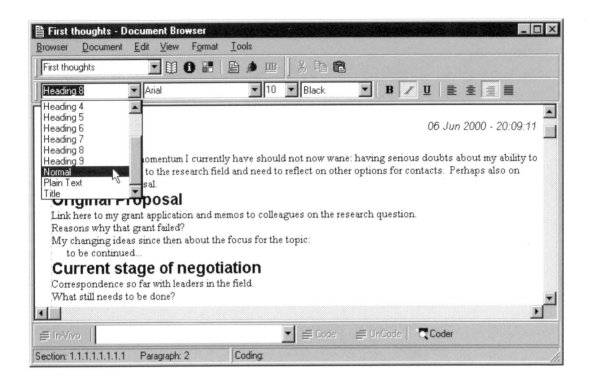

- To make a subheading, place your cursor where you wish to write (or in the text, if it is already written) and select an appropriate style, such as Heading 2, or Heading 4.

- Add emphasis to your text with bold or italics—perhaps bold for keywords, or change the font size. Use a color to mark things you're still unsure of, with a different one for key concepts or for things you already know, or significant questions.

You will now be able to see a clearer path through your text, while aspects that are particularly important and which will need to be reviewed will catch your attention on later perusal.

The Document Browser is a special tool for combining editing and coding. Although it is like a standard word processor, it will not allow overtyping of highlighted text. If you highlight a passage of text and start typing, NVivo will assume the highlighted text is to be coded with what is typed. To change the text, press Backspace or Delete to remove the highlighted passage, then retype.

If you have decided to use the Researchers project, use the instructions above to create a project and make a document in the NVivo editor.

Provide a heading, using Heading 1 style, for example, "Initial thoughts." Insert the date under the heading. You might record ideas about what it means to be doing research, something of your own experience of doing research up until now, why you are researching now and what you want to be able to do with NVivo. Make subheadings for the different things you write about and use the Styles slot to set them at Heading 2.

The start of my project journal is shown in the box below. The first entry suggests the project had rather nebulous beginnings. Even in writing those first comments, I set down ideas, moved away, came back and fiddled, decided to add headings and color, and so was creating a "living" document that changed and was edited as my thoughts developed.

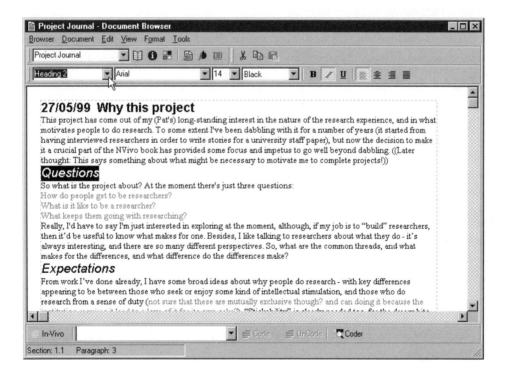

Managing your documents

The Document Explorer in NVivo shows a "bird's eye view" of all project documents and assists with managing documents. Like the Windows Explorer, it shows, in outline, what each document is about, as well as the properties of each document.

Explore a document

- On the Project Pad, click on Explore all Project Documents.

  The Document Explorer will open. In the left pane, the All Documents folder is highlighted. In the right pane of the Explorer your first document is listed, with its size, coding information, creation date and the date it was last modified.

- Double-click on All Documents and highlight the name of the first document.

  On the right pane of the Explorer, the outline of that document will be shown. If a heading has a + sign next to it, click on the + and the subheadings for that section will show. Additional information about the document shows at the base of the Explorer window.

View and change document Properties

The Properties dialogue will allow you to rename your document, to give it a description, or even to change the color of its icon! It also allows you to specify whether a document is a memo.

- Click on the Properties icon, *or,* select Properties from the context menu which is found by clicking your right mouse button.

- Check This document is a memo.

NVivo automatically distinguishes between memo and non-memo documents—something we will find useful at a later stage of the project.

Jump to the Document Browser

To return to the text of the document, or a particular place in the text, ask to Browse it. To browse a document:

- Highlight the document title (anywhere in the Explorer dialogue) and click on the Browse icon in the toolbar 📖 *or,*

- Highlight the document title and select Browse/Edit/Code Document from the context (right mouse button) menu,

The Browser will open where you were last working.

To open your document at a specific section:

- Highlight your document title in the left pane of the Explorer, so that its contents are outlined in the right pane.

- Click in the section you want to view, and choose Browse/Edit/Code from the context menu.

A reminder: press F1 to read more about the dialog you are in, or go to the contents of Help to read about any aspect of the software.

Linking to other data

A Journal will often benefit from being linked to other material, to illustrate or develop the points made. NVivo allows hyperlinks from the text to other related files—files which you don't want to import aren't needed or can't be imported into the project. By making these links you create other "bites" of data within a document—so these are termed DataBites. When a DataBite is created, the text is marked as the "anchor" for the link. A click on the anchor will allow you to choose to jump directly to the linked file.

For example, if you are working on a funded or dissertation project you might link your Project Journal to the formal project proposal. Whilst it is unnecessary to have the whole proposal in the project (and it may have formatting that will not be preserved in NVivo) a link to it will allow access at any stage. Or you might wish to link your Journal to a photo of the first team meeting, a picture of the site for the project, or a clip from the tape of an early discussion about the project, none of which can be saved as rich text for import to NVivo.

Creating a DataBite, linking the text to your proposal

- Find a reference within your Project Journal to the research proposal, and highlight the text where the reference is made. (Highlight at least one character or space, but preferably more so it can easily be seen. It may be useful to edit into the text words that explain what you're linking to, and to highlight those words.)

- Click on the DataBite symbol. The dialogue will ask whether you want to make an internal annotation (an option discussed in Part 4) or link to an external file. Choose to link to an external file.

- You are taken first to a folder provided by the program for storing External DataBites. Navigate through the directories to locate the file you wish to link. Select it, and click Open.

The text that you had highlighted will now appear in green with an underline. This marks it as the "anchor" for a DataBite.

Accessing the DataBite

- Click on the DataBite anchor (the underlined green text).

- Click on the DataBite icon in the Browser's toolbar, *or*, select Inspect DataBite from the right mouse button's context menu.

NVivo calls the appropriate application, which opens the linked file. The project proposal will be opened in your word processor, or the photo in whatever software your computer has for displaying photos. You can edit those files and save any changes made in the normal way.

Note: If you move the external file after making the DataBite, the link to your NVivo document will be broken and NVivo will ask you to re-locate it.

Follow the instructions in the previous section for making a DataBite to link your Journal text to a photo. You can link to an authentic (!) archival record of the authors creating trees in the early stages of Pat's Research Farm. Add a comment about this being a project set up by Pat, highlight it, click DataBite, choose to link an external file, and locate the photo file. It is in Researchers 1\All Users\External DataBites. To see the photo, click in the DataBite anchor then on the DataBite icon on the toolbar.

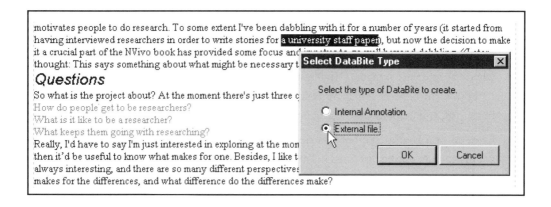

Modeling your preliminary ideas

Often it's helpful at an early stage to sketch ideas about a project. NVivo provides a Modeler to assist in this. You might make a diagram of the relationships or patterns you expect to find in your study, based on prior experience or preliminary reading. Identify things in your journal and use links between them to indicate possible relationships.

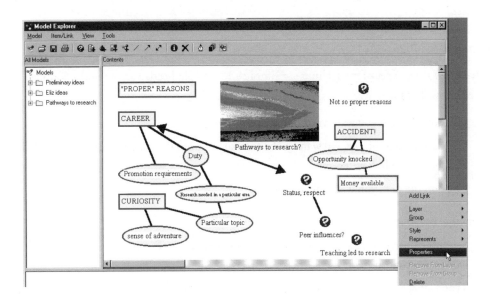

 D.I.Y.

◔ Create a model

- From the Project Pad, select Create and Explore Models. The Model Explorer will open. Expand the window.
- Select New Model (on the left side of the Explorer), click on it again to change to edit mode, and type in a name for the model.

...add items to the model

- Click on the Document icon in the toolbar. Select the Project Journal and click OK.
- A document icon with the document's name will appear in the model. (This is a "live" link to the document: double click on it to see its Properties; or select it and from the context menu choose Browse/Edit/Code Document to see its text.)

- Click on the New Item icon in the toolbar, *or*, select Add New Item from the context menu. A "?" icon will appear in the model. To name this icon to represent some thing, person, place, action, event or other concept, double-click on its label, and type in the name.

- To design the icon, select it and click on the Properties icon in the toolbar, *or*, select Properties from the context menu. Click the Appearance tab to change its color, shape or font.

...then link the items

NVivo offers three types of model links—a simple line, a single-headed arrow, and a double-headed arrow. To link items:

- Click on the item you want your link to *start from*.

- Click on the type of link you want in the toolbar, *or*, from the context menu select Add Link and the type of link you want.

- Click on the item you want the link to *go to*.

...and label the links

- Select the link (it becomes highlighted) and choose to see its Properties (using the toolbar icon or the context menu).

- Type a label for the link into the Properties dialogue. The style or colour of the link can also be changed through this dialogue,.

Move the elements of your model around the screen until you are happy with the layout and appearance of your model. You can also print the model (choose Print from the Model menu), or you can Export Model to Clipboard and insert it into another application.

Try sketching your preliminary thoughts about what leads to someone becoming and staying a researcher, using the Modeler. Draw on your own experience and the ideas expressed in the project document you have created.

Making it safe

For those with full software, there are two different ways of saving a project. The first updates the version of the project you are working on. The second saves a backup copy of the project. It is advisable to do both.

Whenever you feel confident of the work done, you can tell NVivo to save by selecting Project>Save Project from the Project Pad menus. Revert to Saved will return the project to where it was when you last (deliberately) saved the project. NVivo has been auto-saving whilst you worked, and this updates a single copy. You can set how frequently the auto-save occurs (select Tools>Options from the menus at the top of the Project Pad).

For safety you need at least one other copy, regularly updated, as a "back-up" against machine failure (or even researcher error!). Making regular backups for a project is essential. No matter how expensive the equipment, power failures or human intervention can make it crash, and no matter how confident you are, errors occur.

D.I.Y.

Saving the project

NVivo allows you to make a backup copy while you are working in your project, and provides a choice of which copy to continue working on. When you are working in your real project, also make regular backup copies that are stored on *another computer or safe storage medium* (zip disk or file server).

- From the Project menu, choose Save Project As... A dialogue will open suggesting an appropriate title and location for your backup project. The title can be changed, but be sure you make it different from any existing titles (and change the backup Project Folder name to match, as well). You can change the location for your backup also, for example, to another drive or other storage medium.

- Indicate whether you wish to continue working on the current copy, or the new one, by checking (or not checking) the option Close the current project and open the new one.

Note: This process calls for good housekeeping: always keep a record of your backups and their names. When you next open your project, you will want to be sure about which copy you want to continue working in.

Taking stock

The project has started, a first document has been created, and you're under way storing and picturing early ideas for the project. There is of course no requirement that a project start this way, but it's a good way of getting going. All of the methods of qualitative analysis share an expectation that analysis should be ongoing from the start of the project, whether the project is designed to test prior ideas, or to generate new theory. The early hunches and questions are data, informing insights later, critiqued in the light of subsequent discoveries. Understanding and theory evolve, growing out of the data beginning from when the project is first conceived.

Starting this way, you have prioritized your ideas and questions. Data processing tasks won't overtake analytic insights. As this record grows, the journal will chart the history of your understanding of the issues and development of hunches and ideas. You can link it to external documents such as literature summaries or original proposals or to data documents as they are added to the project. You can model those early ideas, display them for discussion and store them for review. The resulting log of your progress will become the foundation of theory tested by or generated from the data, whatever your chosen qualitative method.

Most (but not all) qualitative researchers wish to code data. Coding has both an organizational and an analytic role. It is one way to manage data and store knowledge gained from the documents, or interpretations made. Once stored, coding is easily retrieved. Qualitative researchers have many ways of coding which we discuss later (Part 4). But almost all use coding to identify topics, themes or issues, and bring together the data segments where these occur. When this was done manually, it was a formidable, tedious task. NVivo does it as you think, by making nodes for topics, and storing there the references to text coded at that topic.

Nodes out of data

If you coded manually before using software, you probably did it by making notes or colored marks in the margins of text, or by photocopying documents, then cutting out the segments about a topic to store in (named) files. You could then find all the blue margin marks, by rereading and looking for blue. Or more efficiently, you could go to the container that had all the photocopied snippets, to read everything stored about that particular topic. When you found some more, it was copied and added to the container for that topic.

In NVivo, the "containers" for coding are nodes. You make a node for each topic or concept to be stored. But you code by placing at the node not segments of data but *references to* the data about that topic. NVivo is not cutting documents up or copying that text across to each node. That could be problematic since nodes (like filing cabinets!) would fill up. Also, since a document can be freely changed, the text at the node could be out of date. Whenever you ask NVivo to browse the node, it quickly finds all the text that node has references to. If you change the structure or size of your document, NVivo will automatically update the references it has stored at nodes and find the correct text. More importantly, those snippets are not cut away from the original—you can see them in context, if necessary returning to the whole document.

Coding "up" from your project journal

When writing a first document, you will have mentioned some topics or categories of significance to the project. You will want to capture further data about these, to view all the data on a topic, and to ask questions about how topics are related. Creating nodes for them will allow you to do this.

The simplest way to code "up" from the data is to name the category with a word in the text that is interesting or that triggers thinking. The node named "live" from the text is called an "in vivo" category. Code at that node every time this word occurs, with the context it occurs in, and you can explore its recurrences and meanings. In some methodologies, this sort of coding is paramount. The term "in vivo coding" comes from grounded theory, but of course creating a node from the text can be used in any method, as a quick way of naming a node.

Making In-Vivo nodes

D.I.Y.

- In the Project Pad, click on Browse, Change, Link and Code a Document, to browse your Project Journal; or, Explore all Project Documents and select it and click Browse in the Document Explorer.

- Read the thoughts you recorded in your journal. Find a word or phrase for a topic you would like to develop or explore in your project.

- Highlight the word or phrase.

- In the Speed Coding Bar at the bottom of the window, click on In-Vivo.

- The word or phrase you had highlighted appears, with a Free Node symbol, in the Speed Coding slot next to In-Vivo.

- The status bar immediately below tells you that the selected text has been coded with a node of that name. The location of any highlighted passage also shows in the status bar.

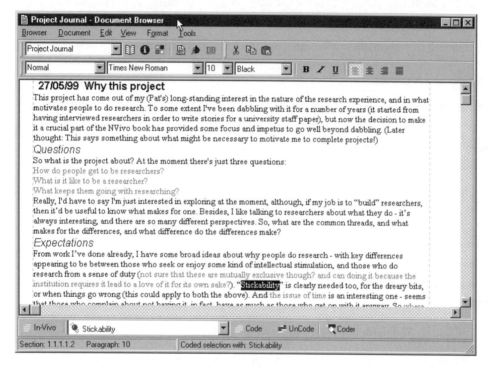

You have created your first node! Note it was created as a Free Node. NVivo provides several types of nodes for keeping track of emerging and developing ideas, and for organizing data. Free Nodes do not assume relationships with other concepts, so they are particularly useful at the beginning of a project. Nodes can also be organized into "Trees" to express relationships of topics and subtopics, or grouped as Cases. These will be discussed in Part 5.

Working with retrievals

Coding using a computer allows retrieval of the text that was coded—instantly! At any stage you can view what is coded at a node in a Node Browser, which shows where the coded text was from, and how much of it there is. The Node Browser looks very similar to the Document Browser, with a Speed Coding Bar at the bottom. This is a different sort of browser, however—not for editing text, but for reading what was coded, for reviewing and reflecting, and perhaps for recoding into finer categories.

Retrieving what you have coded...

D.I.Y.

- On the Project Pad, click on the Nodes tab (next to Documents, near the top-left).
- Click on Browse, Change, Link and Code a Node. The dialogue will list the In-Vivo nodes you have made.
- Double-click the node you wish to view, or select it and click OK.

...and seeing it in context

Hmmm. What you have retrieved is probably just a single word. There will be times when you look at coded text, stripped of its context, and wonder why it was coded there, or what it meant. You can view the immediate context of a coded segment, or alternatively, jump to the source document.

- In the Node Browser, highlight the coded text.
- From the context (right mouse) menu, choose View Enclosing Paragraph.

NVivo will show the whole paragraph, with the additional text in a different color from the words initially coded there. Bringing in additional text like this does not mean that the extra text has been coded at the node—just that you can see more clearly where the extract came from.

If the enclosing paragraph is insufficient for your needs:

- Put your cursor in the coded text, and from the context menu select View Enclosing Section.

This is likely to be as far as you need to go, but if the passage is a sub-section of a larger section, repeating this action will bring in the larger section, and again, until you reach the highest level of section—which is the whole document!

...optionally code additional context at the current node

To extend the coding to include all or part of the context shown:

- Highlight the additional text you wish to code at the node, and
- Click Code or press Enter (the node you are browsing is already showing in the Speed Coding Bar).

Uncoding can be performed in a similar manner.

...or return to the original document

There are many reasons why you might want to go back to the document a coded segment came from—even if the context was adequately coded. Perhaps this segment gets you thinking about the document again? Perhaps you now see how different this person's response was from others' coded at the node? The coded segment shown in the Node Browser was not severed from its place in the document.

- In the Node Browser, place your cursor in the passage of interest.
- From the context menu, choose Browse/Edit/Code Document (the first option).

The full document will be retrieved in a Document Browser with the coded passage highlighted. Now you can rethink, recode, or edit the document as you wish to store your new ideas.

Note the node you came from is showing in the Speed Coding Bar of the Document Browser. So you can immediately code some more text there if you wish:

- Highlight the extra text.
- Click on Code.

The additional text will be coded at the node that was showing in the Speed Coding slot. The status bar will record that you have coded text at that node, and the Node Browser for that node immediately updates.

More Free Nodes

Often you will want to store ideas at new Free Nodes with names that are not in the text. Doing so is delightfully (perhaps dangerously!) simple—as simple as typing a name for the new node.

These techniques quickly create nodes "up" from the data. They are often "eruptions" from the document. They serve to store surprises, hunches, odd phrases, things that might matter. Thus a node serves many purposes. Simply by thinking "that's node-worthy" you create a category. If these things recur, coding at the node will track their occurrences. Now, when you come to more data about the same topic, you will have a place to store it—where you can find it again. Moreover, the nodes you have give a growing picture of what's happening in the project. If they prove of no interest, they can simply be deleted.

Free Nodes with new titles

D.I.Y.

- NVivo will make a Free Node for that category, and will indicate in the status bar that the selected text has been coded there.

This time, when you retrieve the text coded at the node, you will find there is more than just the title of the node stored there.

Coding at a recently-used node

Coding brings material together on a topic. Soon you will find a second passage to be coded at a node you have already created. If that node is not currently showing in the Speed Coding slot:

- Highlight the passage.
- Click on the arrow at the right side of the Speed Coding slot to access a list of Recently Used Nodes.
- Select the desired node from the list, then click Code.

Alternatively:

- Retype the node title into the Speed Coding slot and press Enter on your keyboard. Make sure you spell it correctly, or NVivo will create another node with the misspelt title!

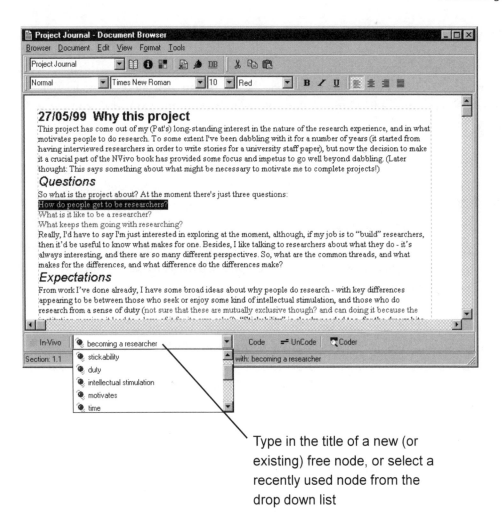

Type in the title of a new (or existing) free node, or select a recently used node from the drop down list

Viewing coding

Once coding is under way, it helps to see what coding you have done! How has this document been coded so far? Or what other nodes code the text you are viewing at this node? You can view this graphically in live "stripes" alongside a document or the text coded at a node in either Browser

View coding stripes

- From the View menu in the Document or Node Browser, choose Coding Stripes. Colored bracketing, with node titles, appears alongside the text, indicating where it is coded, and at which nodes.

- As you add more coding, this will be shown in more or extended "stripes". Note that you will often have more than one stripe against a passage, indicating there are multiple nodes coding that passage.

NVivo's stripes in the live Browsers take a lot of computer memory, so if memory is a problem on your computer it is a good idea to turn them off whenever you are working intensively with a document or node, particularly if you are editing a document or coding on from a node. Turn them on again when you wish to check where you're up to.

Browse through the project journal, and highlight a word or phrase that might be used later to "tag" some data of interest. Click on In-Vivo in the Speed Coding Bar to create a Free Node with that word or phrase as a title. Now extend the highlighting to capture the whole question or comment, and click on Code (the appropriate node should still be showing in the Speed Coding slot). Maybe there are some further nodes you can make in this way. Or you may want to re-use a node you have already created: find it by clicking on the arrow next to the Speed Coding slot to bring up the list of Recently Used Nodes.

Try creating a Free Node by highlighting a passage and typing a title. Click on Code or press Enter on your keyboard. Use Coding Stripes to see what text you have coded, and review the text you have coded at a node by calling up the Node Browser for that node.

Exploring nodes

The Node Explorer offers an overview of all the nodes in a project, and access to those nodes. From the Node Explorer, you can edit the title of a node, record additional descriptive information about a node, or create a new node.

Explore and retrieve

D.I.Y.

- From the Project Pad, select the Nodes tab.

- Click on Explore all Project Nodes.

    The Node Explorer will open. Areas for storing the several types of nodes (Free, Tree, Case) are shown on the left of the Explorer window. For the present we are interested only in Free Nodes.

- Double-click on Free, to see a list of your Free Nodes.

    All Free Nodes are listed in bold type, which indicates that each has coding. The right pane of the Node Explorer tells how many passages are coded at each node, when each node was created and when it was last modified.

- Go to the Node Browser either by double-clicking a node (in the right pane of the Explorer), or (in either side of the Explorer), by highlighting the node title and clicking Browse.

Create a node without coding

Think about another topic you want to consider in this project. You can create a new node while in the Node Explorer, without coding text at it yet. For now, keep all these nodes in the area called Free, as they are free of organization or structure.

- Highlight Free in the left pane of the Node Explorer.

- From the context menu, choose Create Free Node. A new Free Node (with the title Free Node) will be created and highlighted.

- To rename it, click on Free Node (it will change to edit mode) and type in a new title. The new node title is presented in regular rather than bold type, because there is no coding at this node.

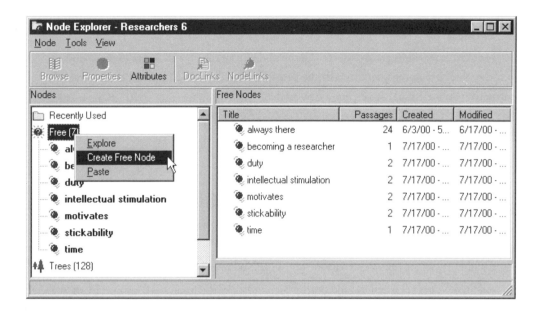

Record a description

You can record a description to define the concept, say why you have made this node, or what is to be coded there.

- While the node is highlighted in the Explorer, or open in the Browser, click on the Properties icon in the toolbar, *or*, select Inspect/Change Node Properties from the context menu (Explorer only).

- Type a description into the Description slot of the Properties dialogue. Note that you can also edit the title of a node through the Properties dialogue.

- Close the Properties dialogue. When that node is selected in the Explorer, the description will show in the lower right pane.

Nodes in models

At this stage you might return to your model, to explore relationships between your original ideas and the nodes you have created from your journal, and to add to or refine your first attempt by using those nodes. The items you put in a model are "live"—with a click of the mouse you can jump directly back to the data referred to.

Adding nodes to a model

D.I.Y.

- From the Project Pad, select Create and Explore Models. The Model Explorer will open on a new model or, if you have a saved project, the model you started at the end of Part 1. Expand the window.

- Click on the Nodes icon in the toolbar, *or*, from the context menu select Add Node. Select the nodes you want, one at a time. As you select each one, it will appear in the model and be added to the list of the model's items in the left pane of the Model Explorer.

- Rearrange the early ideas and added nodes, to picture how they relate to each other and to the Project Journal document you added in Part 1. Add links, and delete or change the appearance of items as required.

- To jump from the model to the document or data coded at any node, from the context menu select the option to Browse/Edit/Code it. The Document Browser or Node Browser opens, ready for more thinking and coding—or just to remind you of what it was about.

The way I modelled with the nodes I generated from my Project Journal is shown below. Already the experience of playing at developing a model suggests to me that managing time and "stickability" may be related to setting priorities – something to think about when I come to doing searches and/or developing a theory (and meanwhile, worthy of a note in my Journal).

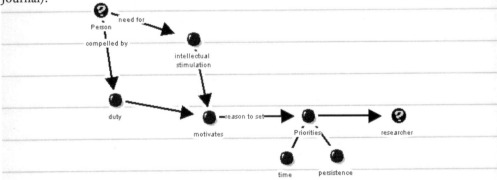

Saving your project

If you have the full software, this is a good time to re-save the project by going to the Project menu (at the top of the Project Pad) and choosing Save Project.

Taking stock

NVivo's database is now quite complex. It contains only one document but also some links, a growing model, many nodes and some coding at them.

Significantly, the database has grown before you introduced any of the sorts of documents conventionally called "real data" (interviews, field notes, etc.). In your own project, you may wish to create more new documents to record your observations, field notes or interviews. Or you may import such "real" data from rich text files: we will do this in the next section. But note much can (and often should) be achieved in the early stages by logging and exploring first thoughts.

In presenting the first stages of a project this way, we aim to alert researchers to the ways NVivo supports what we have learned are crucial reflexive techniques in qualitative research. The software will not stop you if you work in a more linear way, importing all your "real data" in a batch, *then* coding all the documents, *then*, and only then, thinking about the ideas represented in the coding, and the data coded there. But we share an experience of working with researchers that has convinced us that working linearly almost always creates problems for qualitative analysis. If you hear a qualitative researcher ask: "Now I've coded all my data, what do I do?" you know they are in trouble. As they were coding their data there were very many other things they should have been doing that would assist them in drawing conclusions from their data, things that may be hard to regain later.

By contrast, you have created a starter project that is holding and representing what you are learning in several ways. A visitor to this project could find easily how it had started, trail its progress and view its current development. If you continue to work this way, moving between tools to explore and express ideas, the project will be understandable and your conclusions justifiable to your audience—and yourself!

Part 3: Making data

In Parts 1 and 2 you began a project with first thoughts and growing ideas. To do this, a new document was created in NVivo's editor. If data is building up in field notes you may continue to create documents this way. But most projects also require some data documents that were first created in other software—a word processor or database program, or an email provider or scanner. Such documents may be transcripts of an interview or focus group, or copies of historic records or correspondence.

In this Part we make data in several ways; by typing in, by importing and by making proxy documents that represent and link to data. Whichever way you choose to make a document, it is a rich text file, and you can edit it, link it to other documents, files or ideas, store information about it, code it and search it for patterns and relationships in your data.

Early data documents

For documents like those so far in your project, there is little effort and a considerable advantage from having the text in your project database. But such documents need not be restricted to obvious project items like the project journal or interviews. If you haven't yet begun to make data, you can (and should!) still make a start on your project, by viewing the literature about your topic as data. If you have a word processor file on your literature, a download of literature details from a website or library search, or output from a bibliographic database, import it as shown below.

Most researchers create data as they reflect on the research experience, (field notes, reflective notes, notes about reading or observation records). Some researchers have only this sort of data. You may be studying, say, the culture of a professional practice or the movement of a patient through a hospital system. Observations create different sorts of data from recording interviews with professionals. You may wish to start a document called Weekly Observations and type into it each time you note something (dating the entry). When you remember another event, drop back into that document and add to it.

Notes from observations and records of "casual" conversations may be supplemented by interviews or focus groups. (For some types of data, good notes from interviews are likely to be as useful as full transcripts, and they will be a lot easier to manage and absorb.) These too may be typed up in NVivo, or prepared in a word processor.

Edit or import?

How to decide whether to type up data in a program outside NVivo? The advantages of doing so are that word processors have some functionality not present in the NVivo editor, for example, a spelling checker, word count and thesaurus, as well as greater flexibility in using styles. On the other hand, an advantage of typing directly in NVivo's editor is that there will be no compatibility problems, and, as we saw in Part 1, you can code as you write.

If you save a file in your word processor, then import it, you can keep the word processor file as a back-up copy. If it was created in NVivo, you will need to make a text report of it, or go back to it in a backup of the database to find a back-up copy.

Appendix B provides additional notes about preparing documents for easy processing in NVivo.

Importing a document

For documents prepared outside NVivo, a minimum of preparation is required. Documents prepared in a word processor are saved in rich text format in Word if you want to preserve the styles and formatting applied to the text, or they are transferred from other programs via WordPad (note that WordPad preserves formatting but not styles). Documents in plain text format can be marked-up to allow NVivo to identify the name, description and sub-headings (see the Appendix). Any document can be freely edited after it is in NVivo.

A document needs a name. If you are importing, NVivo can take the name from the source file name, or it can be typed into the document. A document can also have a description, and subheadings that define sections in the document, as well as text.

The document name and description can be changed at any time, using the Document Properties box. In the Browser, subheadings can be added at any time, as can further text.

Import a rich text or plain text document into NVivo

- Decide on a document to import: a first interview transcript, a memo to your supervisor, or simply a document written in a word processor for this exercise. Make its first paragraph a description, and use subheadings to identify useful sections (e.g. for questions or speakers). Save it in the Source Documents folder of your project, selecting rich text format (.rtf) or text only (.txt) in MSWord, as appropriate.

- From the Project Pad, select Make a Project Document.

- In the New Document Wizard, select the first option, to Locate and import readable external text file(s).

- Navigate to where your file is located. (If it is a plain text file, select Text Files (*.txt) in the file format slot in order to see it.) Select the file, and click Next.

- NVivo asks how to find the name and description the document will have in the project. Usually for a rich text document you will choose the first option, taking the name from the file and description from the first paragraph.

NVivo will copy the document into its own database, leaving the original unchanged. You may wish to move the original document to a back up area.

View the document in NVivo

- Browse the document: from the Project Pad click Browse, Change, Link and Code a Document and select your document, *or*, from the Document Explorer, select your document and click Browse.

  The Document Browser opens, and you now have live access to the text of the document, to read, edit and code.

Tip To move straight to a particular section of a document: in the Explorer, highlight the document in the left pane, and in the right pane highlight a section heading. Click the right mouse button and select Browse/Edit/Code. The Document Browser will open at that section heading.

Follow the instructions above to locate and import Elizabeth.rtf from QSR Projects\Researchers 1\All Users\Source Documents. Leave the first option selected in the Obtaining document name and description box, so that the source file name becomes the document name and the first paragraph its description. Click Finish.

Open the Document Explorer (from the Project Pad, Explore all Project Documents), and highlight Elizabeth under All Documents. The structure shows in the right pane of the Explorer. Open the document Browser at one of the section headings. From the Edit menu, choose Select Section, and the highlighting will extend to include all the discussion for that section (for both speakers).

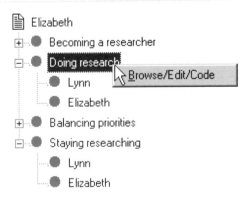

Proxy documents

The third way of making a document is the fastest—tell NVivo to make a "proxy document" for some data you don't want to import, or can't. This can be as simple as a heap of photos, or as complex as a videotape. NVivo offers either a proxy that is linked to a file somewhere else in your computer (by name only), or one for non-file data. And it offers either a blank document or one whose formatting gives you a structure or template to type your summaries or comments into.

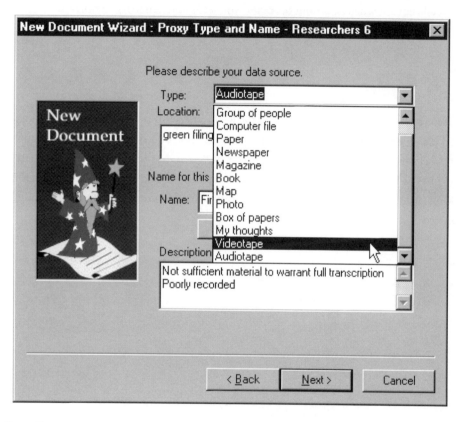

Creating a Proxy

D. I. Y.

Whichever way it is made, the proxy document is a rich text document where you can edit ideas and summaries, place links to external data and code.

If you have data requiring this sort of treatment, for example, a report to summarize, a heap of newspaper cuttings, a set of photographs or a focus group not worth transcribing:

• In the New Document Wizard, select the third option, to Make a Proxy Document for non-file data. Click Next.

• Specify the name and description and click Next.

- The dialog asks if you want a formatted proxy. Choose the option to have numbered paragraph headings and in the adjacent slot, select the relevant one (e.g. for a report, pages or chapters; for a focus group, tape count numbers or minutes). Indicate what the starting and finishing numbers will be, and click Finish.

- The document opens. Type your summary of the report or what happened in the focus group into the relevant places according to chapter or tape numbers—or simply leave the numbered paragraph headings as placemarkers for coding. Use External DataBites to link to small audio or video clips from the tape if you want to retain magic moments!

One of the early focus groups conducted for the Researchers project went on for quite a long time, but did not produce a lot in the way of startling information or insights. A proxy was made, rather than transcribing it all, with some brief excerpts included in the proxy, and others linked to audio "sound bites". (The video recorder—hired at great expense—failed to record! Just as well there was a back-up tape-recorder running.) You can view this proxy document, its links and its coding in Researchers 5.

Attributes and values

There are things you "know" about characteristics of the sources of the data such as people's gender, the dates of events, locations of sites. Such information is contextually relevant for everything that is written or said. NVivo stores this information as *attributes* of either documents or nodes. Attributes can be used to filter and search data. Thus, for example, providing the relevant attributes and coding have been recorded, one could ask whether there is a gendered response to an issue, or whether the style with which something is done differs across sites or periods.

It is easy to set up and assign attributes to documents or nodes, as you work out what information might be useful for later analyses. Or, when this information is known in advance, and applied to many data items, it can be recorded in and imported from a spreadsheet or database (i.e. any table-based software). Importing attributes using a table is outlined below (Part 8).

Attributes are specific to the project. When documents or nodes represent people, demographic details are likely to be attributes (gender, age, role). Where documents are field notes, then their attributes may include place and time. If a project includes more than one type of data, an attribute for data type will allow comparison of what you have on an issue from different sources. If a node codes all the data about a case (see Part 5), it can be given the attributes of that case.

Attributes have values as specified by you. Sometimes these are obvious in advance (gender will have values of female and male). Sometimes new values are created as the data determines (you discover the many different roles of people in a hospital ward). Attributes can be given string values, that is, any word or combination of letters and numbers you type in. Or the value will be Boolean (True or False) for example, for the attribute "Has doctorate"? Age and income (if treated as continuous values) are numeric; "Beginning of event" requires a date or time. You choose the value type.

Document and node attributes are handled identically. If the people or sites you are studying are represented in only one (whole) document for each, assign the attributes to the document. (We will do this in the Researcher project, where each interviewer "is" just one document, and the focus group participants are not studied as individual cases.) But if a person or site is "spread" across parts of several documents, you would give them a node, and assign their attributes to that node (see Part 8).

Creating attributes and values

D.I.Y.

- On the Project Pad, click on Make or Change a Document Attribute.

- In the Create/Edit Attribute dialogue, click in the slot to Type the new attribute name.

- Type a name for the attribute and press Enter (or click Apply).

    Note: If you are creating a Boolean (True/False), numeric, date or time attribute, change the default Value type from String, before pressing Enter.

- Type names for further attributes, choosing a value type and pressing Enter after each one.

- Highlight one of the string attributes you have created. Click on the Value tab.

- Type in the values you wish to use for that attribute, pressing Enter after each one.

- To create values for another attribute, first click on the Attribute tab of the dialogue, highlight that attribute, then click on the Value tab and continue as before.

- Close the Create/Edit Attribute dialogue.

There are always three pre-assigned values for any attribute: Unassigned, Unknown and Not Applicable. These importantly distinguish three different reasons why you may not have the information to record a value. The default value is Unassigned, unless you alter it.

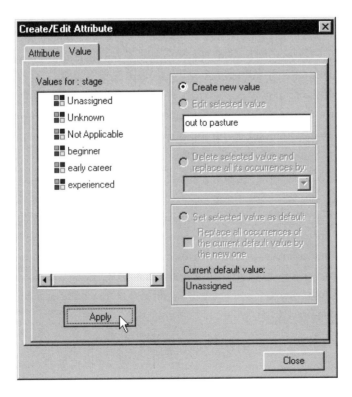

Exploring attributes and assigning values

Attribute data can be added, edited or reviewed at any time. Once Document Attributes have been created, they are available for application to any document.

- From the Project Pad, choose to Explore all Document Attributes. A Document Attribute Explorer will open showing a table that lists all documents and all attributes. "Hover" over a cell, to see the value (for each at present this is Unassigned).

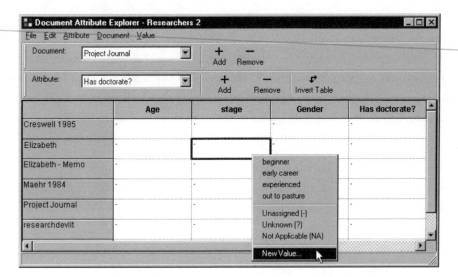

- Click on a cell and click the right mouse button. A list of the values created for that attribute shows in the pop-up menu.

- Choose the value to apply for that cell. If the appropriate value is not available, select New Value, type its name and click OK.

- Continue in this manner for as many cells as you need to fill.

Check the menubar options. You can customize this table, adding or removing from it (not from your project!) particular documents and attributes. You can also sort the attributes by type, or the documents by their values on an attribute.

Values can be entered "on the run", i.e. as you are working through a document, if the information becomes available in that way.

- Select Browse a document

- Click on the Attributes icon  in the Document Browser toolbar. A "mini" attributes table for just that document will open.

- Create attributes and/or add attribute values as they become known.

Elizabeth's document begins with a description that identifies a number of attributes that are likely to be important in considering her development as a researcher. She is an *early career* researcher (this tells us about the stage of development she has reached); she is at *New University* (whether she is at a new, Sandstone or Greenfield university, or in business, tells us something about the research environment in which she works). In addition, we know that she is *female*, and from the text of the document we discover that her discipline area is *social sciences*.

Create Document Attributes for, say, gender (with values: male, female) and stage (values: beginner, early career, experienced). Assign values for Elizabeth using the Attribute Explorer or through clicking on the Attributes button in the Document Browser. View these attributes at any time by accessing them in the same way.

Links to Memos (and other documents)

Qualitative researchers usually want to link documents in their project to each other. This may be simply to remind that another document is related. Or it may be to create and edit notes that record growing ideas about data or concepts or research procedures. These are usually called memos.

Any document may be linked to any other documents, or to any place in the text of a document, by what NVivo refers to as a "DocLink". Documents may also be linked to nodes. "Top-level" links—from one document to another—are mutual, each document showing the link. "In-text" links are just one way, since there may be very many of them.

Creating and using memos

A memo in NVivo is any document to which you give that status . Create a memo by making a new document and clicking This document is a memo in its property box, or, by making a DocLink from an existing document (or node) and clicking Link a New Memo. This is a normal document so if you wish, you can code it too—either later, or as you write it. It can be renamed, described, searched and edited like any other document, and it too can hold links to external data (DataBites) or other documents (DocLinks).

A memo may be a major think-piece about theory, possibly the first document you write, and not linked to any other data. Or, it can be just a reminder to yourself about things that draw your attention, queries raised in your mind, things you want to follow up, *linked* to the data it is about. If you are dealing with interviews you might write a memo about your recollection of the interview situation. It is useful to read quickly right through the transcript before looking at the text in detail, and then to record a memo about key points raised and other thoughts the document has stimulated. Memoing helps to focus attention prior to undertaking detailed analysis of the document, when you can easily lose yourself in particulars and miss the focus of the whole. The summary remains as a reminder thereafter of what that document was primarily about.

Linking from the text to an existing document

In Part 1 you used DataBites to link text to *external* data. DocLinks can link from a place in the text to *internal* documents. At any place in the text you might wish to be reminded of related material, or make a memo. For example, you might wish to record some insights gained from your new data document in your Project Journal, and to place a link there that will take you directly to the new document.

Link text to a document

- Browse your Project Journal.

- Add to it a note about the document just imported. With your cursor at the end of the note (don't select any text), click on the DocLinks icon 📄 on the toolbar.

- A box opens entitled In-text DocLinks from [document name]. All project documents show in the left pane. Select the one you want to link to, and click the arrow to show it in the right pane (Documents linked). Click Close.

The DocLinks icon now shows in the text.

- Click on it and right mouse button to see what's linked there (or to return to the Add/ Remove dialogue).

- To go to the linked document, select it and left-mouse click.

Linking a new memo

Sometimes the appropriate link is not from a place in the text but from the document at the top level, for example, to link to the whole document a memo about it. When you place a DocLink you are given the choice of whether it is at top level or from a place in the text. In either case, there is an option to link to a new memo. Choose this, and a new document is made. The default name given to the memo (e.g. Elizabeth - Memo) reflects both its source and its special status as a memo. You can, of course, change that name. You can also change the status of the document so it is no longer a memo (via the Properties dialogue).

Creating a memo

- Select your data document in the Document Explorer.

- Click on the DocLinks icon on the toolbar.

- The dialogue is set to Show top-level DocLinks.

- Select Link a New Memo. A new Browser window will open, titled [Your-document-name] - Memo. (Note: This is another way of making a new document!)

- Type any questions or preliminary understandings of processes which were prompted by reading this document.

- Close the memo. Close the DocLinks dialogue.

- The new memo is now listed in your Document Explorer, with an icon showing it is a memo 📝. It is a full status document, so can be renamed or given a description. To do this—or change its memo status!—select it in the Document Explorer and click Properties. Note that in the Properties dialogue, This document is a memo is checked.

Accessing the memo

- Access the memo from the Document Explorer in the same way as any other document: select it and click Browse.

- To access the memo from the Document Browser, click on the DocLinks symbol (or select DocLinks from the context menu), Show top-level DocLinks, and Browse Document. *Or:* Switch to the memo by selecting it from the Document List in the slot at the top left corner of the Browser's toolbar.

- You can access the original document from the memo in the same way. The memo and the original document have the same status as documents and the link is symmetrical. Each "knows" it is linked to the other.

 Tip You can create a top-level DocLink from the Browser too: just click the DocLink icon and click Show top-level DocLinks, then proceed as above. But note that for top-level DocLinks the icon does not show in the text: if you wish to be reminded that there is a memo about this document, simply edit that into the top of the document! You can of course create an in-text DocLink at this note to allow you to jump immediately to that memo. NVivo will allow any number of links to a document from the top or from any place in the text.

Having read the document "Elizabeth", record your overall impressions of the themes and issues raised in a memo for Elizabeth, following the instructions above. Keep in mind the key questions for the project—how did Elizabeth come to be a researcher, what is her experience of being a researcher, and what keeps her researching. You might note her changing views of what research is about, and query how important the research environment during her early years was for her development as a researcher.

Taking stock

Your project in NVivo now has a database that is complex but relatively orderly. As the data documents "come in" you can record things you know about them and ideas you have about them. You could keep building data up in this way for some time without losing the immediate knowledge and first responses that are critical in qualitative work. Some researchers will continue to work this way for most of the project; their strategy is to gather material with regular, rigorous storage of information and ideas. But most researchers will want also to record the ideas that come to them about particular pieces of data, and the categories that "emerge" as they read the data. To do this, you are likely to want to do more detailed commenting, linking and coding. Part 4 is about working with data using these tools.

This Part describes processes of thinking "up" from the data. Central to qualitative method is the combination of ways of recognizing, recording and exploring ideas discovered in data. Central to the design of NVivo is the goal that many ways of recording of insights and ideas can be integrated. If you wish to edit or annotate, you do not have to stop coding and go into another mode. If you code, it is not invalidated by subsequent editing. Memos happen as ideas form, and can be coded. New nodes happen as a result of coding, and the nodes you have made already can be revised and enriched as you move around a document. You can rethink them as you use them and code memos that discuss them.

Reflecting and recording ideas

Annotating text, memoing specific points in the text and writing memos about documents or nodes are different ways to record ideas about the data, typically undertaken concurrently with coding, not as different stages. As you become familiar with these tools, reach for the appropriate one to record an idea.

Annotating the text

Some reflections on the text are brief notes, aside comments. Others are reflections on the detail of discourse or the use of a term, or reminders about a related item. As you read, minor, brief insights can be inserted "behind" the text of the document, using DataBites. DataBites are the DataLinks that take you either to data external to the project or to annotations.

Internal annotations are fast to prepare and fast to access. Click on the anchor and see the annotation. They will appear "live" in text retrieved by coding; they can be printed as endnotes on a text report of your document, but their text can't be separately coded or searched.

Link an annotation

- Highlight the text you wish to annotate.
- Click on the DataBite symbol in the Browser's toolbar.
- Confirm that you wish to make an internal annotation.
- Type your note in the box provided, then click Save & Close.
- Note that the text anchor for the DataBite has been marked.

To access your DataBite:

- With your cursor in the marked text, click on the DataBite symbol, *or* choose Inspect DataBite from the context menu.

DataBite anchors are text, not an inserted icon. This allows you to highlight just the text being annotated (the expression discussed, for example) or to insert a note which is developed in an internal annotation ("argument followed") or a description of the linked external file ("this is a photo of Annie"). The anchor should generally be quite short (a word or phrase rather than a whole sentence or paragraph).

Elizabeth makes some comments worthy of at least a brief note right at the beginning of her story. Why does she choose to comment on our choice to include her in our sample? What is the significance of her continuing references to the role of her parents in her educational and employment choices? These notes might be recorded as internal annotations.

Memoing detail

There are times when a specific comment in the text prompts reflection—something that is said gives clues to the process being studied, or spins thinking off in a new direction, worthy of a memo linked to that text. You can create new memos, or keep adding to a memo created for the document. If it will be helpful, the memo can be coded or further links made as you write.

If the reflections you wish to record are more about the category (node), you can link the memo directly to that node as well as to that point in your document. Or you may wish to make a new memo for the node. Text (with its coding!) can be copied and pasted from one document to another.

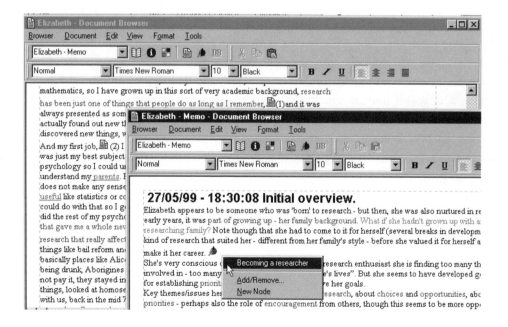

Link a memo

While working through the text, when a word or phrase or sentence prompts reflective thinking:

- Place your cursor at the *end* of the passage of interest.
- Click on the DocLinks icon in the Browser's toolbar.
- The DocLinks dialogue appears, set to Show DocLinks from the selected text position. You can now link to a new or existing memo.

Tip

NVivo has many ways of logging the history of your ideas. Insert the date and time in your memo (select from the Edit menu). Use a subheading to identify each addition to an existing memo. Use the ability to edit a document to insert an identifying number or letter into the text immediately after the DocLink icon (your cursor will already be there), and identify with that number the specific entry in the memo about that text. Or the text that prompted the comment can be copied from the Document Browser and pasted into the memo, for detailed analysis there.

For many researchers the key to qualitative coding is to combine it smoothly with reflecting on data. Coding becomes an analytic process, rather than a mechanical sorting of text. Coding memos as well as the original text will redirect your attention to the issues you've raised and your reflections on them.

Elizabeth's document is rich with recollections and dialogue "demanding" reflection by the analyst. What does it mean, for example, for research to be seen as a "normal" everyday activity? For education to be "useful"? Her critical change in perspective on the nature of what research is warrants reflective comment, as does her realization that, for her, research "has always been there". Also of interest is her assertion of the need to be "ruthless" in claiming time for research.

Coding and what it does

Coding has both an organizational and analytic role. Some knowledge about the content of documents will simply be descriptive. Which of the research questions is this about; to whom were the speakers referring; what event were they describing? But some of what you "know" will be interpretive, concepts that are derived from the material in the documents—labels to express how this person is coping; what this comment is telling me about the context of what's happening here; the impact of that event.

In what follows, we start with some advice on coding for researchers unfamiliar with qualitative coding. Then we outline how to do it in NVivo, coding either from the Document Browser (as you focus on a document) or from the Node Browser (as you review a topic).

Thinking about coding

Coding is a way of expressing thinking "up" from the data: it makes nodes, and gathers references to the material about these topics. You can then review all that material, think more about it and code on from it.

Coding is also a way of thinking "down" from categories to all the material about them. You can access that descriptive and conceptual knowledge, refine it, check back to the original context, and (as will be shown later) explore or test conclusions by checking for associations between those concepts, descriptive categories and/or ideas. So, organizationally, coding is a useful way of keeping track of topics or ideas, and of documents about those topics. But more than that, creating a node and selecting text for coding are interpretive, analytic processes in which thinking about the data is extended beyond the descriptive to a more abstract level. These processes lead you in different ways—to thinking about the shape of your categories, to thinking about the many sorts of material at that category, to asking questions about relations of categories.

Initially coding is likely to be of four (not mutually exclusive) types:

a)   In Vivo coding in which you pick up words, phrases and ideas directly from the text. In Vivo codes are likely to be much more about detail and some will later be dropped or merged with other codes.

b)   Descriptive coding which captures information provided in the text, such as where or when an event may happen, what someone reports about how they are feeling. While some of these descriptive categories may be further explored in terms of the conditions and consequences applying to them, minimal interpretation is required at the initial point of coding.

53

c)   Broad-brush coding gathering material on wider categories. These might be topics of questioning or observations, whole responses to structured questions, or key themes or issues arising from the data. Later, as the relevant dimensions become clearer, you can return to these nodes and use the live Node Browser to "code on" this material into more discrete categories.

d)   What we will call concept coding, where you are using the code to pick up and "open out" an idea that you might want to explore. At this stage these concepts might be broad or detailed, descriptive or interpretive. Memos are often useful in association with this type of coding.

Approaches to coding

In the introduction to this book, we highlighted the range of qualitative methods, and warned that the researcher must find a relevant method for their research question. Coding will be very different for different approaches to analysis. Some work through data in broad-brush mode first, then concentrate on more detailed coding and analysis of particular themes or issues. For example, a field researcher may first identify the formal groups or institutions in the setting studied, then return later to everything coded at this "obvious" topic, more finely coding evidence of informal structure, cultural patterns, etc. In other methods, researchers work very slowly and reflectively through documents, coding as a way of developing concepts. In grounded theory studies, for example, researchers may work by "open coding", going through early documents line-by-line and memoing extensively as a way of "breaking open" the data and the concepts held therein.

Your approach will be shaped by the nature of the project and the structure of the data, and these in turn by your methodology and training. But almost all methods involve coding, and many ways of coding. If you are uncertain about how to code, or, more critically, why you would want to do this, return to do more general reading on methods. Once you locate your study methodologically, the uses of the variety of techniques will become clearer. But whichever approach you take, it is crucial to remember that coding is just one way of working qualitatively with your data. As you code, use other ways of stimulating and storing ideas—visual clues (highlighting the text), linking, memos and models also to capture the rich ideas prompted by your data.

Broad-brush coding

Given the live Node Browser, there is no need ever to treat coding as permanent. Rather, treat it as a first step to thinking something out. As you read through the document you will find that there are larger passages (perhaps whole paragraphs or speaking turns) you can code at broad topic areas (themes, issues, such as you identified in your project journal or the document memo). Possibly these are already identified as sections in the document, because there was some structure to your data gathering. It may be useful to code (name) these topics/themes/issues simply as a first pass. This will bring some level of organization, particularly important if the volume is increasing. It will give access to all the data coded at one topic, e.g. all the answers to Question 3, or everything Jim said. A review of the codes developed this way will give an overview of the range and depth of topics covered. Furthermore, this kind of coding allows examination of the context in which a code is used. For example, does it make a difference to how the respondent discusses a particular issue if it is in response to the question asking about that issue, compared to when it comes up spontaneously during discussion of another topic?

It is quite possible, too, that early coding proliferates categories. Broad-brush coding will allow you to identify text that is particularly relevant to the area/s you need to focus on for now. Once you have conquered those areas (and delivered the thesis or report!), you can return to analyse and report on those topics set aside.

One of the tutorials in NVivo, *Get on with living*, shows broad-brush coding at work. The researcher, Lynn Kemp, coded her interviews with people with spinal injuries first at very broad categories (e.g. community services, employment, education). She then "coded on" from the community services text (which was her immediate focus), capturing the detail of what it was that people with spinal injury were seeking from life, what services were offering, and how these might be redesigned to allow their clients to fulfil their "plan of life".

Concept coding

By contrast, for some methods, analysis involves detailed exploration of early ideas, with thinking about all of a concept's possible meanings recorded in codes and memos. What results is a highly integrated process combining development of codes, coding, memoing and reflective journaling. Concept development happens fast in this approach and the first documents coded will strongly influence the categories developed to capture that thinking. So methods which involve creating categories "up" from the data require ways of checking the recurrence of early categories and of ensuring that new categories can be generated from later data, with the possibility of checking back through earlier data for those later concepts.

A pragmatic approach

If you are unfamiliar with these techniques, a useful in-between way to start generating codes is to identify interesting passages in your text, and create a code (or multiple codes) that "tag" it. The node title might be descriptive, only later being changed to something more abstract and of use also in coding other documents.

Try the following three steps which Lyn developed for undergraduate teaching: many of us have found they lead to generating useful codes. (If you are very unsure, print the document and work first on paper.)

Identify: What's interesting? Highlight the passage.

Ask: *Why* is it interesting? This may generate a useful descriptive code or perhaps an interpretive code. Make a node (or on paper, write it in the margin).

Then ask: Why am I interested in *that*? This will generate a more abstract concept that will be of general use in your coding system, particularly when one starts to organize the concepts/categories into a more structured system. Make a node, or a paper note. And so on to the next interesting passage.

The immediacy and convenience of doing this on screen will soon win you over from paper coding! But either in NVivo or on paper, what happens is that nodes are "emerging" from your thinking about the data—and at the same time you are connecting them to the data about that concept.

As you create a code, get into the habit of documenting what it is. Name it carefully, and if the title doesn't provide clear identification, add a description. If the code is at all interpretive or abstract, record in a memo what made you see this as a category, and what you were seeing in the data you coded there.

You can print a report of all your nodes and their descriptions at any stage, providing a detailed "codebook" to review and rethink, and to use as you code.

Coding in NVivo

Once you start coding, many things happen at once. It is important to see them as research acts—as part of the process of analysis. One is making nodes (saying you are interested in *that*), a second is putting at the nodes references to selected text (just *this* is interesting, and about *that* topic). A third is visiting the node to see what's there, maybe recoding it, or coding on. While this early momentum is building, it's easiest to use Free Nodes for holding coding.

The process of thinking about a code will sometimes also prompt a memo, and similarly, the process of writing an annotation or a memo can assist in clarifying what codes are needed—so the processes work best when they are integrated. At first it will feel that progress is slow, but soon the project is growing simultaneously in several areas, and they are linking in a web of data, categories and thinking.

In what follows, we focus on the coding processes in this web of interpretation. We describe coding from the Document Browser, but note, exactly the same processes apply if you are coding from the Node Browser.

Develop ways of recalling your research questions (e.g. in the Project Journal). It is amazingly easy to become beguiled by fascinating "red herrings". But also be aware that red herrings may indicate rich fishing fields for concepts as yet undeveloped—perhaps this "irrelevant" idea should be stored, just in case it becomes relevant later?

Coding at new nodes

When something is interesting, decide *why* it is interesting and why you are interested in *that*. These questions will tell you whether you want to annotate or code. If you want to make a category for *that*, think coding.

Using the Speed Coding Bar

- Highlight the passage of interest, and think about the categories required to do justice to this passage. It probably needs several.

- Create new nodes either by In Vivo coding or by typing a new node title. For now, allow them to be Free Nodes: in Part 5 we will begin to shape them into a more efficient system.

- Think carefully about what the passage is saying: *what* it is about (descriptive type codes), *why* it may be important (analytic type codes).

- Consider also whether it might be useful also to write a memo related to the nodes you have created (especially the analytic ones).

New nodes can proliferate in this early stage, but as themes recur in further documents, it is more common to be re-using existing nodes (see below). If re-use doesn't happen, worry! The categories may be too specific to apply to more than one document. Or the data may be too atomistic to give a general picture and synthesis of what is being studied.

Coding at existing nodes

If the node needed already exists, there are several ways to find it quickly and select it to take the coding of a highlighted passage.

Recently Used Nodes

- Select a recently used node from the Speed Coding slot and click Code—as described in Part 2.

Use the Coder to work with nodes

- Click on Coder in the Speed Coding bar. The Coder will open to the right of your document, showing Free Nodes already created. ("Jiggle" this around the screen, to get it in a position allowing access to the Browser's scroll bar.)

- Select a passage and click on the Free Node you wish to code it at. Click on Code at the bottom of the Coder.

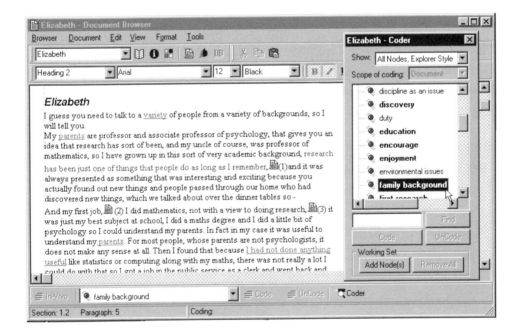

Drag and drop coding

- Having highlighted a passage, select a node in either the coder or Node Explorer. "Drag" it to the passage (or drag the passage to the node). The cursor will show a "no go" symbol ⃠ until it is on a highlighted passage, or a node, then a "drop" ⤵ sign to indicate it has reached "home."

- The node title becomes bold showing there is coding at that node. If that node is selected in the Coder, the text coded at it is highlighted in the Browser.

Tip Selecting the text to be coded can be speeded if the selection is to be a whole sentence, paragraph or section. From the Edit menu of the Document Browser, choose to Select Word, Sentence, Paragraph or Section. *Alternatively,* a double-click will select a word, and four rapid clicks in a passage will select the whole paragraph.

Checking Coding

Qualitative coding often requires reflection on previous coding, not merely processing of more data. An overview of coding in either Document or Node Browser can be obtained by viewing coding stripes, but you can also check what has been coded at particular nodes in more exact detail.

D.I.Y. *Use the Coder to review coding*

- Open the Coder.

- Click on any bold node title (bold indicates that there is coding there for the open document). The exact text coded at that node will be highlighted with a teal color, or with red if the text is also selected.

- Interested in what's coded at that node from another document? Select any Recently Used Document from the slot at the top left-hand corner of the Document Browser. Click once on it and it will open in the Browser. Any text already coded at the node selected in the Coder will be highlighted.

If you have so far resisted the temptation to go to the node, now is the time!

Coding-on from a node

At a node are the references to all the text you have coded there from any document. So browsing a node shows you the data in a quite different context—that of the category, not the original data source. In Part 2 we saw that the context of the coded segment is always available. But so too is going *on* from the first coding, to rethink and develop your coding. All the coding facilities available for documents are also available in the Node Browser. So at any stage when you are considering the material you have coded at a category, you can code on to new or existing categories.

Browse and code a node

- Browse the node of interest (select it in the Node Explorer and click Browse)

- Reflect on the material coded at this category. It's likely to be an odd collection, since you have not yet refined the meanings of your nodes.

- Use the normal methods of coding, exactly as in the Document Browser, to code this material on to further existing categories.

- Use the methods for making new nodes to create finer categories to express the subtler interpretations you are now making.

You just did something quite extraordinary. Before they had a live Node Browser, qualitative researchers could not code-on and so reshaping coding involved a much more complicated process of making notes about desired changes and then returning to the documents. Later we will use the ability to code-on as a way of developing categories from early "broad-brush" coding or from the results of a text search.

Because topic headings have been included in Elizabeth's transcript, these can be used to speedily code major sections of the interview to nodes for <u>becoming a researcher</u> and <u>being a researcher</u>. Doing that will allow the question to be asked, say, about whether encouragement from others was spoken of as being helpful in the context of becoming a researcher or of being a researcher? And did those who provided encouragement vary in those different contexts?

To undertake some detailed coding and analysis, try going through Elizabeth's document concurrently making internal DataBites, writing or adding to Memos, coding text. Some parts of the document will end up being more heavily coded and annotated than others (especially the first section). Much of the text will be coded more than once—create and use nodes freely, as necessary or useful. You might wish to add further DocLinks to your memo for Elizabeth, or to new memos, or to link memos to nodes.

Coding a proxy document

The processes outlined above for coding and reviewing coding apply equally to coding of a proxy document. The only difference is that when coding the proxy document's text, you can code references to units within the original source. The proxy document can include additional notes, memos and DataBites as well as pre-formatted references to e.g. tape count or page number. Retrieval of coding of a node will show all these details, including the unit of the original source coded there, and will offer the usual access to linked documents and annotations.

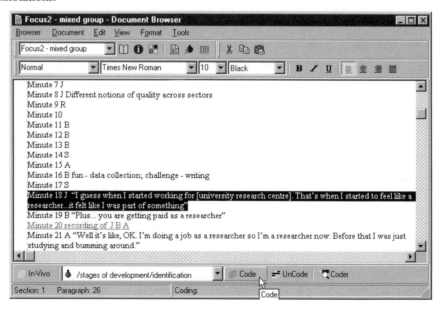

Avoiding pitfalls in coding

The multiple tools provided by NVivo encourage the analyst to think about each document in detail whilst also making links, making comparisons and identifying commonalities. The results of that thinking are recorded in codes, memos, journals and models. These tools help you to move beyond "disposing" of data into coded segments, and to begin to see patterns and process. The contexts of coded segments are always available, and thinking about coding is always ongoing. The danger is that coding becomes a seductive task, a way of moving through data and gaining a sense of achievement, but also, to some extent, a way of deferring thinking about the data. Maintain the discipline of memoing ideas generated by the data, and of journaling thoughts related to the project as a whole. It is useful always to read quickly through a new document, to get a sense of what this document is about and to record that, before thinking codes. And then to say at the end, "Well, what did I learn from that?" Because you're thinking about the participants and the concepts being generated, other experiences, other conversations, other snippets from previous reading are recalled. Consider these, and if noteworthy, record that in the Project Journal.

Reflections on a document

Having imported and coded a document, you might wish to reflect on what you've learned so far in answer to your questions. There are several ways to do this. By reporting on documents and nodes you can review progress. You can add further comments to the memo for your document, or in your project journal. Or you can sketch new insights as a first component of a new model.

Making a text report of your document

For many reasons you may want a report of the document *out* of NVivo. If the text was edited in NVivo, you may wish to save the new version as a word processor file. You might wish to make a report (perhaps showing coding stripes) to include in a project discussion. The text of your DataBites and details of other links can be shown as endnotes to the text report. Or you might want a report of your document with paragraphs and sections numbered. After coding, this will allow you to quickly see the overall structure and where, within that, text retrieved at nodes is coming from. Before engaging in on screen coding, you might want to take this type of report and sit under a tree, away from your computer, and scribble on it as you read, deciding on coding and memos.

Making and printing a report

D.I.Y.

- From the Document menu at the top of the Document Browser, choose Make Text Report.
  Or: In the Document Explorer, highlight the document name, and from the Document menu choose Make Text Report.

- Choose to Show DataLink details as end-notes.

The document will open in a new Text Editor. Any internal DataBite annotations will be listed at the end of the text (in full), along with any references to external DataBites or to memos (without the actual text). If the default options were unchanged, the sections and paragraphs of the document are numbered.

- From the File menu choose Print, or click on the printer icon in the toolbar of the Text Editor.

Saving the file so that it can be opened in your word processor

- Rather than print, from the File menu in the Text Editor, choose Save As.

- The Save As dialogue will open with Text Files (*.TXT) showing in the Save as type slot at the base of the dialogue. Click on the arrow to reveal and select Rich Text Files (*.RTF) as the format for your report, if you wish to preserve its formatting.

- Provide a name for the report file. Note that NVivo defaults to its own Reports folder (C:\QSR Projects\[your-project]\All Users\Reports) when you choose to save a report. It's useful to save reports there in the first instance to avoid losing them!

- The report can now be opened in your word processor.

Printing a report with coding stripes

- In the Document Browser, from the View menu choose Coding Stripes.

- From the Browser menu, choose Print. Click OK. (Note: there is no option for limiting the size of print or the number of pages to be printed.)

- To change the paper size or orientation, click on Properties in the Print dialogue before clicking OK. Adjust the options on the Setup and Paper tabs in the Properties dialogue as needed.

Warning: Page settings have been set to default to US letter: if you use A4 you will need to change these.

Reflecting in a model

By reporting documents and reviewing nodes you can reflect on the shape of your project. By editing memos or a journal you can capture ideas developed through working with the document/s. But it helps also to be able to draw, and sometimes re-draw developing or changing ideas about the processes that are occurring. In Part 1 the Modeler was first used to draw preliminary ideas about your project, using items created within the model. In Part 2 nodes from your journal were built into the model. The tools discovered there can now be used to sketch what has been learned from your first document.

As you work through your documents and ideas develop, change the model, add to it, add it as an item in a later model, or simply store it as a record of your thinking at this stage.

D.I.Y.

To create a new model

- Open the Model Explorer and expand the window.

- From the Model menu, choose New. A New Model will be listed under Models on the left side of the Explorer. Click on New Model (or highlight it and click on the Properties icon) and type in a name for your new model.

Adding items to your model—a reminder

- Click on the Nodes icon in the toolbar or choose Add Node from the context menu. From the dialogue, select the nodes you want, one at a time. Drag them around the screen, thinking about how you would want them to relate to each other.

- To create an additional concept for the purposes of the model, click on the New Item icon in the toolbar (or access from the context menu) and double-click (or chose Properties) to name the new item.

- Add in a document—linking in memos about particular ideas can be useful.

- Add links between the nodes/concepts/document on your screen, to show relationships between them. Choose to see a link's Properties to add labels or change its appearance.

Develop a model based on critical elements in Elizabeth's becoming and staying a researcher. Try to move beyond the specifics of her case (such as research oriented parents), to what might be more general principles, for example, incorporating such things as exposure to research, intention, way of thinking about research, personal qualities needed.

The Source Documents folder for Researchers 1 holds three further documents. The document 'Researchdevlit' contains literature or other reference material gathered over some years prior to the beginning of this project. These were recorded in a bibliographic database (ProCite), and the document is a direct export from there of the citation information plus the Notes and Abstracts fields for each reference. They have been configured so that in NVivo each reference will become a section of the document, with the author and date as the heading for the section. Creswell 1985 contains notes taken from Creswell's extensive review of the literature on factors which enhance research performance, while Maehr 1984 is a theoretical article about achievement motivation. Because of the length and coverage of these two, they have been set up for NVivo as separate documents, using author names and dates as titles. These are included in the project as they provide data on the range of concepts and ideas being discussed more widely around the themes

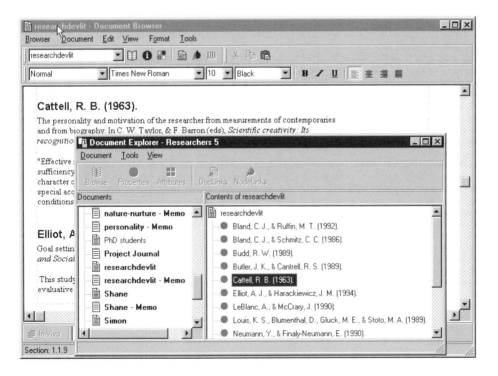

of developing academic researchers and building up (or predicting) faculty research performance. Note how headings have been used so the vital author and date information needed for writing up literature will be easily accessible from the Document Explorer. These documents provide further sources of data for the project.

Taking stock

At this stage in a project, you can seek a sense of momentum. The project is under way. You should be able to reach for the tool you need to record or locate the idea, the insight, the links, the connections that are starting to emerge from the data you are now handling in detail. As you get more surefooted, these will feel less like techniques used in sequence and more like thinking aloud. The ability to code in different ways, and to code on from the results of your coding, opens significant new paths to analysis. Having worked through one or two early data documents, you may find you need now to change the pace of your processing of data, as data gathering often gains momentum. A snowball sample behaves like a snowball, growing alarmingly as it rolls on. Entry into the field is suddenly facilitated. You need tools for moving data into the project fast, without damaging it. Broad-brush coding allows you to code now, rethink later.

Just as the project is now underway, so too your system of thinking about the data is integrating. At this stage, the research process should seem driven by the data and the ideas generated by the data, not by predetermined sequences. And the project should start to seem like or develop as a web of interconnected data and ideas, not discrete parts. Now you can start to shape the project as a whole, so you can manage the data more skillfully, and do greater justice to the ideas you are crafting into embryonic theories.

A major message of the previous section was that NVivo's tools can be used concurrently, so the process of exploring data need not be a process of picking up one tool, then putting it down and starting with another. Rather, as you become familiar with the toolkit, many things can happen at once. Moving now to detailed analysis of a second, and probably a third data document, you will find it easier to integrate these processes. The discipline of careful reading, memoing and coding establishes a framework for considering further documents. This process is greatly helped by good "housework", as documents and/or nodes start fitting together. Documents can be grouped to differentiate different sorts or sources of data. During the routine established with your first data document—annotating, linking, memoing and coding—a coding system begins to "emerge". This involves no magic: it is simply the result of your synthesis, as you see categories and subcategories going together. You may also want to group some nodes—ones often used in combination during coding, or to facilitate viewing coding.

In this Part you will begin to use NVivo's tools for organizing nodes in Trees and documents and nodes in Sets, to manage and shape them as a support to the processes of coding and reflection.

Creating more documents

For the tasks in this Part, you need at least two documents! You may have been concentrating until now on only one or two documents or have created or imported several. Researchers (and methods) differ in the pace of data making. For some methods it is appropriate to undertake detailed examination of each data document, building up ideas from it, before deciding where to go next and how to interpret the next data items. For other methods, rapid accrual of data can accompany broad-brush coding and later revisiting of patterns. (Check which your method requires.)

Create or import a further document, or more than one, noting its attributes, as relevant for your project. If you wish, record any insights gained from a rapid reading of the document in a document memo.

Nodes in Trees

As you work with the detail of a further document, as well as creating new Free Nodes you are likely to find that you want to create a node as a subcategory of another node, or to place it under a more general concept. Free Nodes have no subcategories, but can at any time be moved into places in Trees. In the Researchers Project, references to <u>education</u> or past <u>work experience</u> were each references to aspects of the speaker's <u>background</u>. If they are brought side-by-side under that more general category, the researcher will be alerted to different dimensions of background experiences, possibly adding further subcategories. Again, in the data explored so far, Elizabeth and her family were seen to view research activity in different ways: research was seen as <u>discovery</u>, and as something that <u>really affected people's lives</u>. These could be seen as two dimensions (or subcategories) of <u>images of research</u>.

NVivo allows for the creation of Tree Nodes which can be hierarchically structured with categories, subcategories and any number of sub-, sub-categories. Just as directories and subdirectories in your computer filing system help you to organize your files, Tree Nodes help to organize your categories into conceptual groups and subgroups.

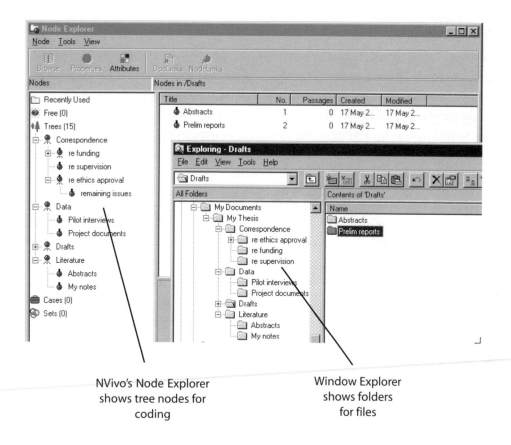

NVivo's Node Explorer
shows tree nodes for
coding

Window Explorer
shows folders
for files

You can use the hierarchical organisation of nodes for any purpose. (In the example above, node trees indicate sorting of categories exactly like those managed in folders). NVivo, like NUD*IST 4, uses the languages of horticulture and of the family to describe these relationships between categories. (Pat reckons this is because Lyn is a family sociologist who likes gardening! Lyn retorts that this language is regularly used in index systems.) A tree has branches and, in horticulture or library index systems, the points at which it branches are termed nodes. A node and its subcategories can also be referred to as a parent with children. Thus, in the Researchers project, background would be referred to as a *parent* node, and education as a *child* of that *parent*. Work experience also is a *child* of background, and a *sibling* of education. In NVivo, the way of recording the full family (hierarchical) title of education, in this case, is /background/education. Every node is therefore identified by both its specific title and its family location.

In Part 7 we return to ways of organizing concepts in tree-structures. For now, the emphasis is on managing nodes as you need them for coding.

Coding with Tree Nodes

Most researchers are greatly helped by working with trees to make the nodes easy to find and logically ordered. The arrangement of nodes is, of course, flexible, so that the trees can be rearranged to reflect changed perceptions and growing understanding. At first it can be useful to make generous use of Free Nodes, so as not to jump too early to a structure, but there are times, too, when structure is more obvious. Location of nodes in Trees often occurs when you go beyond a descriptive category to think about why you are interested that category—the broader concept becomes parent to the particular.

When you use Trees in NVivo, they help clarify the logical relations of concepts. Such clarification is helped by a principle of one-code-one-concept. So, for example, if the text is about a researcher's encouragement from colleagues, it is clarifying to code this text at two nodes, expressing that these are two different *sorts of concepts,* colleagues and encourage. These may later be organized in two separate trees. Colleagues are people (or actors), while encouraging is something people do, so might go into an actions tree. Perhaps, if you are focusing on the issue of encouragement as you write a paper, you will want to see all of the text to do with encouragement (from anyone) together. Or you may want to search for occurrences of another theme, for example conflict of roles, anywhere that the text is also coded for encouragement. With separate nodes for each concept *and the application of multiple nodes to the text*, you can use the Search Tool to answer those questions, or to find all the times it is, indeed, colleagues who provide encouragement (and when they don't!). By contrast, if one code had carried the two concepts (e.g. "encouraging colleagues"), these more subtle questions could not be asked. Perhaps, even, the possibility that not all colleagues encourage would be overlooked!

At first it is challenging to remember all the tools you can use while still thinking about the data, but there is no requirement to make use of all of them yet. As you code, keep in mind that you can also use memoing, internal DataBites and coding as ways of recording your thinking about what it is saying. With practice, helped along by a little patience and a lot of inquisitiveness, you will find you reach for the tool you need for each purpose. And the coding tool will become easier to use as your growing list of ideas becomes organized into Trees of nodes.

D.I.Y.
Create a Tree Node in the Speed Coding bar

- Having imported a new document, open it in a Browser.

- Highlight the passage to be coded.

- Type /parent/child (substituting your names for parent and child, e.g. /background/ education), and press Enter.

As with Free Nodes, your typing will appear in the Speed Coding slot, and NVivo will create a new node and code the highlighted passage to it, but this time it will be a Tree Node. The node icon in front of it is blue, rather than violet.

- To check out where the new node is located, open the Coder.

- Scroll down to where you see Trees. Double-click there, and it will expand to show the new "top-level" Tree Node you have created.

- Click on the + next to that and the subcategory, or child node, will show underneath it. (If you select that node, the text coded there will be highlighted in your document.)

Create a Tree Node without coding

- Highlight Trees in the Coder or Node Explorer.

- From the right mouse button menu, select Create Tree Node. A new Tree Node will be listed under Trees.

- Click on the title of the new node (Tree Node) and type in a new title for it.

- To make a child of that node, highlight the node and from the context menu, select Create>Child Node.

- Rename the node, as before.

Coding at existing Tree Nodes

- Highlight the passage to be coded.

- Select the Tree Node in the Coder or the Node Explorer, or from the list of Recently Used Nodes in the Speed Coding bar. *Or,* type its full hierarchical title into the Speed Coding slot (including slashes).

- If you can't find the node wanted, type the first few letters of its title into the slot near the base of the Coder, and click on Find. The node will be shown, highlighted.

 Don't press Enter during this process. Highlighting text and typing into the slot then pressing Enter is a quick way of creating a new node!

- In the Coder or in the Speed Coding Bar, check the desired node is selected, and click Code. *Or,* in the Coder or Explorer, drag the node to the highlighted text, or the text to the node.

You can, of course, continue to make and use Free Nodes during this process, and you *may* choose to do so exclusively until you have finished working through several documents and developed a strong "feel" for the structure of the data. Or even, if your nodes are few, forever! If you find you've created the same node as both Free and Tree, don't worry too much—they can be moved around and merged without loss of coding as you continue to work.

Open the **Researchers 2** project. An interview with Frank is located in the Source Documents folder for this project at C:\QSR Projects\Researchers 2\All Users\Source Documents. Choose to Make a New Project Document, then locate and import it. Frank is a much more experienced researcher than Elizabeth, and a much more straight-down-the-line academic researcher. Indeed, he is rather more in the pattern of Elizabeth's parents than Elizabeth. This contrast will assist in the development of new categories.

Having imported the text of the interview with Frank, read it straight through to gain an overview of what was said. Start, as before, by making a top-level linked Memo about Frank, record relevant attributes (he's male, and an experienced researcher), then delve into coding and annotating the text. You may find it useful to create some Tree Nodes, for example, for the various people that he refers to (supervisor, family), the personal traits he demonstrates (e.g. commitment, enthusiasm) or the strategies he adopts (e.g. creating a niche, time management) as well as using existing Free Nodes and creating new ones to "tag" freshly revealed aspects of the life of a researcher.

Moving nodes

Inevitably, with the creation of Tree Nodes, you will want to move some of the Free Nodes already created. Perhaps in seeing that this category belongs with that, you will have created the same category as both Free and Tree Nodes, while other existing Free Nodes clearly have a place in the new Trees (colleagues belong alongside family and supervisor as a sub category of people, for example). Nodes can be merged or moved to allow for flexibility and development in thinking about them, as well as to maintain clarity. Cutting and merging a node will remove a duplicate by combining the text references that are at the source node (say, at the Free Node) with those that are at the target node (the Tree Node). Cutting and pasting a node allows for a Free Node to be moved into a Tree while retaining all the coding at it.

The Node Clipboard will hold only one node at a time, so make sure you have placed the node you cut before cutting another! If you feel insecure, use Copy rather than Cut, but then you will need to go back and delete the original after you have successfully placed the copy.

Cut and Merge a node

- Working in the Node Explorer, select (highlight) the node you wish to merge with another (the "source" node).

- From your right mouse button (context) menu, select Cut.

- With your left mouse button, select the node you wish to combine it with (the "target" node) by clicking on the node's icon.

- From the context menu, select Merge Node. Check in the Merge Nodes dialogue that you have identified the correct nodes. Click OK to indicate that you want to transfer the coding and links of the node you are merging.

Cut and Paste a node

- Working in either the Node Explorer, or the Coder, select the node you wish to move.

- From the context menu, select Cut.

- Select the tree (or branch) you wish to move the node into, and from the context menu, select Paste. It will be placed as a child of the selected node.

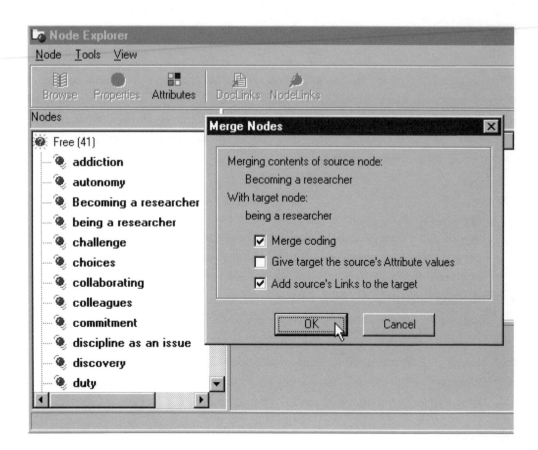

Sets of documents

Most projects have heterogeneous documents—this is the nature of qualitative data. Document Sets help in organizing and managing data sources by grouping documents that share common features. Sets provide a quite different way of managing data from coding. Whereas coding brings together *segments* of documents about a topic to enhance understanding of that topic, sets bring together documents that share some feature. You can filter sets, changing them at will, you can work with sets to shape your research processes. Sets are particularly useful when it comes to searching data, making it possible to limit the scope of a search to just the required documents.

Sets can be part of the research design, planned for use throughout the project. Or they can be quite temporary—constructed, perhaps redefined, then deleted, according to the need of the researcher. It is likely that any document will end up being in more than one set. For example, a field researcher, or an archivist, may wish to create sets of documents relating to particular sites. In team research, different team members may wish to create sets of the particular documents they have been working with, to allow for separate analyses later. In the Researchers project, early data was derived from existing interviews with researchers and notes from the literature, so Document Sets to hold each of these will distinguish them from each other or from, say, focus group or survey documents that may be introduced later in the project.

NVivo automatically creates two sets—memo and non-memo documents. When you make a memo document, it is automatically placed in the memo set. Other sets are established by the researcher—and added to quite simply—in the Document Explorer. Or they can be created much more subtly at any time by using the Set Editor to filter and select documents. The Document Explorer is adequate for now.

Make a new set in the Explorer

D.I.Y.

- Open the Document Explorer, and expand the list of All Documents (or have them showing in the right pane of the Explorer). You will see there is now quite a collection of several sorts of documents—your Journal, the document(s) you have already coded, literature or field notes you recorded, memos you have created.

- Highlight an interview (or another kind of document you have been working with), and drag it to the Sets area, below All Documents. Confirm that you do want to Create a new set using [document].

- Double-click on Sets, to see your new [Untitled] set. Click on Untitled Set, and name it, e.g. "Literature" or "Interviews". Note that the set contains not the document you dragged to it, but an alias for it. The document itself is still listed under All Documents.

- If other documents belong in the set you have just created, highlight them and drag them there. Otherwise, create a further set for those documents.

New documents, or others you create, can be added to this set when they are brought into the project, simply by dragging them to the set icon. The same document can be in any number of sets. You can multiple select documents listed in the right pane of the Document Explorer.

Both of the data documents imported so far are (partial) transcripts of interviews. It will be useful to identify interview documents and to distinguish them from the literature documents by placing them in a set. In the Document Explorer, drag either Frank or Elizabeth to the Sets icon. Name the new set Interviews, and then drag the second document to the Interviews set. You will now see aliases for both Frank and Elizabeth in the Interviews set. Similarly, a set can be made for the three literature documents.

Make a new set in the Set Editor

You may wish to make a set by more subtle processes of selection. Qualitative work may involve bringing together, for example, all of the documents with a certain feature, or those not coded at a category.

- On the Project Pad, select Documents and Make or Change a Document Set. The Set Editor for documents opens. It has two panes so documents can be copied from one set to the other. The left pane will show the set of All Documents by default while the right pane will display the Working Set.

- If necessary, click on the right pane to make it the active pane (white, not grey), then Select All and Remove to empty the Working Set.

- In the left pane, select any documents that you wish to add to a new set and click Copy>> to add them to the Working Set. Those documents will appear in the other pane.

- To make a new set of the items in the Working Set, click the Save As icon at the top of the Set Editor and name the set.

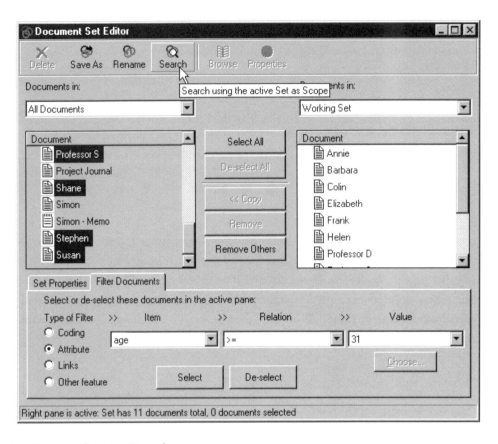

Using Sets to direct a Search

Sets of related documents can be used for many purposes. One of the most useful is to restrict the scope of questions you might ask. This is most important in qualitative work, since it allows you to point a search to just some data. For example, you might want to ask, "What do I have on a topic in my own notes (or from the literature), and how does it compare with what is said in the interviews?"

To ask what you have on a topic usually requires simply browsing the node. But even early in a project, you might like to ask the subtler question of what you have in a particular body of data. To set the scope for any question, you go to the Search Tool.

⌒ Meeting the Search Tool

- From the Project Pad, choose Search Project Database to open the Search Tool. It has three panels, in which you can specify three things; the operation, the scope of the search and how the results should appear.

- Click on the search operation buttons 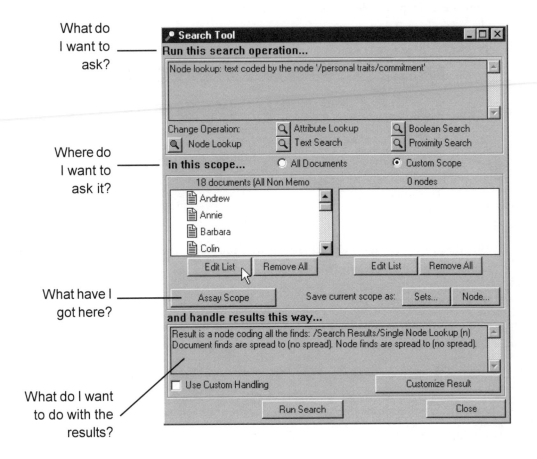. The first three are simple—just looking up a node, an attribute or particular text. The two on the right side offer a range of more subtle searches, the logical Boolean ones or ones about proximity.

- Click on the buttons in the second panel. NVivo allows you to "scope" a search to particular documents or nodes. When you ask for a Custom Scope and choose Edit List, you are taken to the Set Editor to edit a special set of documents or nodes for the search.

- Click on the 'Customize Result' button in the third panel and you will see that NVivo will code the results of your search at a node you select, with any "spread" of context you request.

What do
I want to
ask?

Where do
I want to
ask it?

What have I
got here?

What do I want
to do with the
results?

Specifying and scoping a search

For now we need the simplest search, just the text at a node. But we want it <u>only</u> in memo documents.

Run this search operation...

- From the operations, select Node Lookup. You are asked to Choose a node. (Choose one where you have coded material from your own notes.) Click OK.

...in this Scope

- Choose Custom Scope. Below the list of documents, choose Edit List.

- You are taken to the Document Set Editor. Here you could make a working set for your scope, choosing just the documents you wish to search. But if you already have a set of documents for the scope you want, you can simply select it. From the pull-down list above the active pane, select the set of All memo documents. Only memos now show in the active pane. (If there are none showing, it is because none of your documents have the property of being a memo!)

- Click the Search icon at the top of the Set Editor. You are returned to the Search Tool, with your node lookup still specified but the scope now showing only your memos.

...and handle results this way

No need to change this; the default is that NVivo will code the results at a node it will create under Search Results.

- Click Run Search. A Search Completed dialog indicates how much text was found, and that those finds have been coded for you at a node. Click OK to Browse Node and you will be shown everything from your memos coded at the node you looked up.

To check what's in the interviews, you can simply alter the scope of the search. Select the appropriate set (e.g. all non-memos) in the Document Set Editor. Then, click Search to be taken back to the Search Tool with the new search ready to run.

Sets of nodes

During the early stages of a project, in particular, you will find you are constantly rethinking your nodes, sometimes prompted by modeling and often by new text. A node captures a particular thought, and then as you work on you find a related theme or concept. Should it be placed in the same node as the first, or in a new node? Or should it be a subcategory of the first node? Often the answer is neither—these nodes merely have "something to do with" each other. To organize them in the catalogue-like Trees is inappropriate. You need a node set.

Like documents, nodes can be shaped into Sets, for any purpose. The set expresses no necessary equivalence or logical relationship. It may merely be a way of keeping together all codes to do with a particular issue or context, or all nodes created on Tuesday or by a team member. Node sets can be used for coding, to scope searches, or perhaps to define a set of nodes to be shown as selected coding stripes. The processes of making them are symmetrical with document sets.

 Make a new set

D.I.Y.

- Highlight one of the nodes you wish to use in your set and drag it to the Sets icon.
- Expand Sets to see your new Untitled Set. Highlight it, click again, and type in a name for the set.
- Drag further nodes to the set as required.

 Tip

If the document you are coding repetitively requires a particular combination of nodes, you can use the Coder to make a node set for coding. Coding at the set will then code at each member node. Keep them as a Working Set just for the course of that document, and then click on Remove All in the Coder when coding is completed. Once a set is named, the only way of removing it is to open the Node Explorer, select it, and choose Delete Set from either the Tools or context menu.

Use a node set to view coding of selected nodes

Perhaps you have already created a number of nodes around a particular theme, and you want to see how they relate to each other. If these are in a set, you can easily gather (copy) all the text coded by them into a new node. The new node can then be displayed with coding stripes to show what has been coded by any or all of the target nodes. This will help you decide whether to keep these as separate nodes, or whether to combine them as one.

Construct the search

- Use the Node Explorer to create a set of the nodes you intend to include in your search.
- From the Project Pad, choose Search Project Database to open the Search Tool.

Run this search operation...

- Select Boolean Search. From the dialogue's dropdown list (next to Operator:) select Union (Or).
- Click on Choose Nodes. In the dialogue find the set you have just made, then click on Members to Add the nodes to the pane on the right of the dialogue. Click OK. The nodes you have selected will now show in the Boolean Search dialogue. Click OK. Details of the search operation you have set up now show in the top panel of the Search Tool.

in this scope...

- Click on Custom scope. Choose to Edit the list of documents.
- In the Document Set Editor, choose All non-memo documents, or a particular set of data documents you wish to use for this search.

and handle results this way...

- You will not need custom handling.
- Click Run Search.

View the results of your search

- Choose to Browse Node. All text coded at any of the selected nodes will be shown.
- From the View menu, choose Coding Stripes. Stripes for all nodes will be shown.
- From the View menu, click on Select Coding Stripes... then double-click on Sets, then once on your new node set to select it. NVivo will now show only the stripes for nodes in that set.

Now you can clearly see whether one node codes entirely different text from the other, or whether, where and how much they overlap. It is then up to you to decide whether the nodes should be maintained as separate entities, or combined—or treated in some other way.

Print the results of your search

- As an alternative to printing a text report of a node, print directly from the Node Browser, with the coding stripes shown on the page next to the text.

- Have the Node Browser open and showing selected coding stripes.
- From the Browser menu, choose Print. Click OK. (Note: you will not be given options about how much you wish to print).

I became somewhat caught up with ideas around addiction to research and identification as a researcher when working with Frank's data (partly also because of my own experience of research, and how I have conceptualised that over the past decade or so). Having coded text at each of these nodes, I used the search with selected coding stripes technique to examine the overlap in these concepts—also to answer a colleague's suggestion that they were the same thing. While there was overlap in the results, I also noted that text coded at addiction went further than that at identification as a researcher, and was more emotional than identification. I retained both nodes, and started to think (in phenomenological terms) about emotional responses and intellectual responses as different dimensions of the experience of research.

Cases shaped in nodes

It is becoming apparent that NVivo often gives access to data via nodes and sets. To shape the project, gather material up or distinguish different sorts of data, the choice of tools is usually between coding at a node, and gathering material in a set.

A final shaping task may remain if your sources of data come untidily across more than one document. For example, speakers in a focus group are scattered across a transcript, yet you may want to identify all the text belonging to a particular speaker. Case studies in education will include multiple documents or bits of documents about particular schools (where a school is defined as the case), or each class being studied, or students being followed through a course (where students are the cases). If the data for each case was a clear group of documents, you could make a set for each, but it isn't, so how to link all these sources of information for each case being studied?

Rather, identifying cases and viewing these as belonging to case types allows you to gather together everything about a case *and* to have your data organised in several different ways, if that is appropriate to the study. So, if your study does involve repeated interviews with children going through school, you might have Pupils as a case type, with each interview for each pupil coded at a case node for the pupil under that, perhaps along with their teacher's comments about that child, the researcher's observations, and samples of their work. And you may also have Schools as a case type, with the pupil data from each school coded, along with curriculum and policy documents, to a case node for that school. Pupils could be treated either as an entirely separate case type, or as cases within specific schools (thus making school X a case type for the individual pupils of that school).

If data for cases are spread throughout parts as well as whole documents, code each case's data at a node, where it can all be brought together. This is the reason for having a special area in the Node Explorer for Cases. Coding everything about each case at one node will facilitate asking questions not only about that particular case (within-case analysis) but also about all the cases of that type (across-case analysis). A further advantage of this arrangement is that attribute information can be recorded for both Case Type nodes and Case nodes, allowing attributes to be recorded for part documents as well as whole documents.

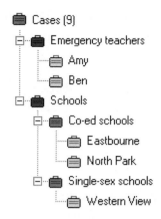

Creating case nodes

- In the Node Explorer, click on Cases. From the context menu, choose Create Case Type. A node with a blue "case" icon will be placed in the Cases area.

- Click on Case Type to edit its title (e.g. to Participants, or Schools).

If you are working at just one level of case analysis (e.g. for participants), then:

- Highlight the Case Type node (Participants) and select Create>Case from the context menu. A green case icon will be placed under the case type node. Edit its title so that it is named for one of the cases in your study.

- Repeat this action for as many cases as you have in your study.

If you are working at more than one level of case analysis, (e.g. at both the level of schools and of particular classes or pupils), then:

- Highlight the Case Type node (Schools), and select Create>Case Type from the context menu. A node with a red "case" icon will be created. Repeat this action for as many cases of that type (schools) as you have in your study. Edit the title of each red case type node to name the cases at that level.

- Highlight a red case node, and select Create>Case from the context menu. Edit the title of this (green) case node to the name of the particular case within that case type. Repeat for each case within each case type.

Note: You cannot create further nodes under a case node. If you find later that you want to reorganize your cases under an intermediate case type, this can be simply achieved:

- Create the new case type nodes.

- Click on a case node, then drag and drop it in the case type node where it is to be located. It will be moved so that it now appears under that case type.

Coding at case nodes

If the node is already created:

- In the Document Browser, highlight the text and code in the normal way (use Ctrl A to select the text of a whole document) using the Coder.

To create the case node at the same time as coding at it:

- Highlight the text and type the name of the case type and case nodes in the Speed Coding slot using periods and colons to identify the level, thus. Case Type.Case Type:Case (e.g. .Schools.Penrose:Julie).

Giving attributes to case nodes

Revisit the ways of creating attributes and values (Part 4). Nodes are given the values of attributes in exactly symmetrical processes to those used for documents. If you are using case nodes, you may wish at this stage to give them attributes representing what you know of the cases (e.g. gender, age).

If you have a lot of cases, it may be better to concentrate on the detail of your data for now, and defer organizing it into case nodes until later (Part 8), when we show you ways of working faster with your data.

Taking stock

Each of the ways of shaping data so far explored creates changes in your project. The database changes when you place documents in sets, and nodes in trees or sets. These changes can be used in further working with your data. None of course are permanent; sets can be rapidly deleted, altered, filtered or re-formed. Trees can be shifted and reshaped. Each shaping tool gives you a different sort of access to data. (Compare with modeling, which offers an opportunity to explore your data visually, to see how your picture changes when you move, hide or group ideas, without impacting on the project database.)

At this stage in a project, the tools available can be used to make it yours—not in a sense of ownership but in a sense of familiarity and belonging. By shaping the data the way you want it, you can become more sure-footed as you explore the increasingly messy and sometimes alarmingly burgeoning data. The goals are variously (for different research styles) familiarity and control, elegance and symmetry. Whatever your metaphor, shaping should bring the data together, in ways that encourage ideas, rather than smother them.

The tools in this Part are tools for synthesis and order, but they should promote, rather than prevent, the development of the data and the emergence of ideas from it. Use the shaping tools all the time, not in dramatic occasional campaigns to win dominance over the data, but in constant conversation with the emerging themes and their relations. Aim for a sense that you know your project, can **see** and **tell** its shape. (Lyn thinks in terms of being able to put your arms round it.) If documents are hard to access, or you forget a group of nodes, shift to shaping again for a while. Now if someone asks you what your project is about, you are likely to be able to answer in less than an hour!

Part 6: "Emerging" theory?

In this Part, you will *not* learn how to create a theory from the data in your project! Qualitative theorizing is highly varied. Different methods do it differently and indeed have different meanings for "theory". And in none of them does theorizing happen in a particular sector of a project, or as a result of particular processes using a particular tool. The theory will not be in this or that part of your project, but in the way you make sense of it.

All methods, however, require analysis—examination of the data in order to understand it as a whole. Getting to that understanding always requires moving beyond description to analytical categories and ways of exploring them, that is, abstraction. This Part is about tools and techniques for abstracting, and ways of handling project data and using NVivo in such a way that you are assisted in theorizing.

What are you aiming for?

You may not see the desired outcome of your project as a "theory" if your goals are pragmatic ones like evaluating a teaching initiative, or understanding how members of a minority group see their situation. "Theory" may seem too grandiose a term for what you will be offering when you get there. Such studies look very different from, for example Grounded Theory studies, whose explicit goal is new theory, "grounded in" data.

If you are unfamiliar with the goals of qualitative theory—or if you are unsure where you are trying to get to in this project—we urge you to read explanations of what theory is sought and how it is constructed in the literature of your chosen method. This book, on software tools, is in no way a replacement for the books on method and studies using your method.

How will you know if you get there?

Theories appear to "happen" in odd places. Most qualitative researchers have stories of the "Aha" moment when the data made sense or things "fell in place". (Preliminary analysis of a subsample of these suggests that high mountains and showers are particularly propitious locations!) Getting to a computer in such locations is never easy, but software may be totally irrelevant in these moments. Rather, splendid eruptions of understanding are always the outcome of prior work with the data. The qualitative literature is replete with references to theory "emerging" from data, but in our experience, theory does not "emerge" without the agency of the researcher. You have to "emerge" your theory!

Theory emergence and theory construction

It is here that NVivo can help. In what follows, we will use terms coined by Barry Turner: theory emergence and theory construction. (Turner, B.A.,1981, Some Practical Aspects of Qualitative Data Analysis. Quality and Quantity. 15, pp. 225-247). The terms nicely distinguish two processes rather than two recognizable stages. (Most qualitative research processes are not neatly ordered in stages.)

Theory *emergence* refers to the process of generating ways of thinking about the data—categories, concepts and ideas—that come from interpretive reading and reflection. What is appearing at this stage is often very unimpressive, a mess of guesses, questions, notes about surprises or small hunches and mini-explanations about what is going on. In our experience as researchers and supervisors, the challenge is always to recognize in this primeval sludge the elements from which theory can evolve.

In theory *construction*, the researcher is creating bigger ideas from the little first categories and hunches, locating the categories that matter, abstracting from them, exploring their relations and crafting an account of the data that offers not just a description of what was found, but an analysis.

Since these are very varied processes, almost all of the tools in NVivo's kit can contribute at some stage to theory emergence and construction. But some are particularly appropriate for the essential processes of theorizing. Since it is your data, and your understanding, how you use these tools and how you make the project work will be a matter of your judgment. At this point the metaphor of the craft is highly relevant; the excitement (and sometimes terror) of this sort of research is that no matter how good the tools, the outcome depends on the researcher's crafting of theory. But it does help to know what tools are available!

A theory is not a node (though a node may be reviewed and reframed, creating finer precious categories that will later link in a theory. It is not a memo (though many a memo has turned into a final chapter!) and not a model (though a layered model might first show you there is a theory here). It is not the results of a search (though that may mercilessly dispose of your current theory or blessedly validate it). Your theory is the way your understanding works to make sense of your data.

There are many ways in NVivo of maximizing the chance that you will discover, retain, review and rethink categories, see themes, recognize recurrences, and work with these atoms of theory in such a way that they move the project from description towards analysis. Once categories are gathering and linking, the researcher can more directly embark on processes of theory construction. The software offers other ways to draw connections, play around with patterns and pursue hunches until they arrive at tested and explained conclusions. Those tools are the subject of the rest of this book.

Exploration of categories

In this context, you may wish to revisit and critically evaluate some of the processes that started your project. In Part 2, with the first coding, categories "happened". In Part 3, as documents were introduced and information about them stored in attributes, the project acquired another way of thinking about the data. Already questions could be asked and models drawn, and surprises uncovered. The techniques of working with data in Part 4 were very obviously techniques of category generation; handling coding and memoing with these tools, you inevitably create nodes, and the software stores these awaiting your discovery of more relevant material, new nuances in an established category, redefining it or rethinking of its significance.

Working in a node

As you work through the text from further documents, you will be constantly challenged to think about the nodes you're making and using. As you scan your list of nodes, ask of each what does it represent? Does it adequately reflect the concept currently being shaped by the data? Are there several concepts there, or several dimensions of one? Is it particular to the document it came from, or does it point you to something more abstract you are interested in?

The first step may be to review the text already coded at that node. Reviewing the text of a node gives a sense of how the node is working by bringing data together into a new context. Thinking about that node in light of new text will help to determine the next step. Should you create a different node for the new text? Or simply modify the existing node title and description to absorb the fresh "twist" in the data? In the process of making these decisions, you are beginning to emerge ideas, and perhaps clarity, as to what your project is about and where your analysis might be going.

The material at a node can be reviewed in two ways—make a report of it or browse it. At this early stage you may wish to print a text report and take it away from the computer to read and scribble ideas. But if you work on paper, ensure that the ideas come back to NVivo (even if they merely record puzzles) and are recorded there. And importantly, recognize that the paper report is only a step to the review that can be conducted in the live Node Browser.

Print the text of a node

- In the Node Explorer, highlight the node you want to read, *or*, have it open in a Node Browser.

- From the Node menu, select Make Coding Report...

- Choose the Document or Document Set to show coding from. Select All Documents, or double click Sets to select a particular set of documents. The latter will limit the node report to segments from just those documents. Check which options you want for your report.

Section and paragraph information are automatically provided at the start of each segment. Selecting section and paragraph numbers will mean they are also shown beside the relevant text. If you choose to show DataLink details as end-notes, the text of internal DataBites will be printed, and cross references will be given to memos and nodes which are linked to specific points in the text.

- From the File menu in the report window, choose to Save As and/or Print the Node Coding Report generated by NVivo. If you choose to save it, make sure you select Rich Text Files (*.RTF) in the Save as type slot at the bottom of the Save As dialogue.

Browse and review the node

An important next step in most theory emergence processes is to start thinking about and working with the category. The Node Browser's tool-kit makes it possible to flick between three ways of thinking of a node, and all contribute to theory emergence.

- Browse the node, and read it as though it were a document.
- Think first about the node as a whole. A useful trick is to look for surprises. You may be surprised to find how much or how little is there, or how inconsistently you have used the node. Are there surprises in the variety or similarity of material coded there? What else is the text at this node coded at, and is this of interest? From the View menu, choose Coding Stripes and reflect on the overlap of this category with others.
- Then secondly, look at the node a different way, reflecting on each coded segment. If its relevance is not evident, drop back to contextualize it, either by viewing the paragraph or section in the browser, or by jumping to browse the source document. This may prompt new discoveries in the source document (annotate it whilst you are there). With the context of the segment displayed, you may wish to widen the spread of text coded at the node.
- Now thirdly, for each of the segments, ask if it is appropriately coded. Should it be here, at this node? And what of its other coding? For a broad picture, choose Coding Stripes again. For a finer indication of the exact characters coded at different nodes, open the Coder. From the pull-down list at the top of the Coder (Show:), select List of Nodes with Coding. A click on any node will reveal which segments (or parts of segments) are coded at that node. Select a particular segment of text (or part of it) and, in the second slot at the top of the Coder, change the Scope of Coding to Selection. Only those nodes coding that selection will be listed.

Naming and describing

You might now firm up the node. Its properties include its title and description: Have you been using these? Both can be changed very swiftly, and as the category firms in your understanding, altering its title and description will record this firming.

The node title can be edited to reflect more accurately what the node is about. Use the node's description field to record how it is being used now, or to signpost concerns about the way the node is developing so that you remember to check it again after another document or two.

Change the node title

D.I.Y.
- In either the Node Explorer or Coder, select the node title you wish to change.
- Click on it again, to change the text to edit mode.
- Type the new title.

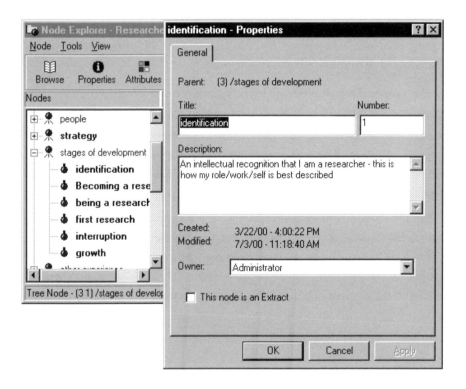

Modify the node description

- From either the Node Explorer or the Node Browser, choose to see the Node Properties using the icon in the toolbar, or by selecting Properties from the context menu.

- Type into the Description slot: Indicate how you are using the node, perhaps say that it now "includes xxx", or flag a concern with a brief query. Click OK and the dialogue will close.

- In the Node Explorer, you will need to refresh the screen before you see any change. The description will appear in the lower right pane of the Explorer.

Note that the Properties dialogue allows you also to change the node title.

Notes on a dialogue: Lyn and I have been talking about use of descriptions, and the processes of refining and locating the nodes so far simply stored in Free Nodes. Her technique is to describe them as they start "earning their keep" in Free Nodes; for example she would now have tentative descriptions of all the Free Nodes that are about "strategy". As those descriptions change, the node firms up and it becomes more evident where (if anywhere) it belongs in trees. So the description is a first step to placing it. I tend to work the other way: place the node first, then if the meaning is not evident, or in dispute, I'll record a description and change it as the meaning is clarified. You might like now to experiment with both ways of exploring and clarifying the Free Nodes building up in **Researchers 3**: describe and locate, or locate and if necessary describe!

A web of ideas

In the process of reviewing a node, you may find you digress from coding to modify the nodes you have already created—to merge nodes, or perhaps to "code-on" to further nodes. As these processes come together, they will give welcome indication that your nodes represent project ideas, not merely atomistic categories particular to one document. Moving from thinking about a document to thinking about a node becomes natural and easy, and with every such move the project is shifted slightly from description of the data to analysis.

Using NodeLinks, you can also link this category to any number of memos, which are full status documents. Use a memo to log the process of development of any node that seems likely to be important in the emergence of your theory.

As these ways of playing with the data become familiar, most researchers use them constantly. It takes only moments to experiment with another subcategory, or explore the dimensions of one created earlier. If this is mere doodling, you may wish not to take time to reflect on it. But as with most theory emergence processes, the best advice is to assume it is never *mere* doodling! When in doubt, take the moment to note in the memo the thought that flitted past!

Reflecting in a memo about a node

As the node is developed, it often requires a memo and as the memo develops, it can hold the story of that category. Depending on your method, this may be very important for validating your theory later. In many qualitative methods, the claims for theory require that the researcher can tell the story (often referred to as an audit trail) of how a category "emerged", was developed and explored and became part of the theory constructed.

The process of creating and recording reflections in a node memo is symmetrical to making a top-level document memo (as in Part 3). Each involves making a DocLink. But when a node is linked by a DocLink to a memo, there will also be a NodeLink (see below) from the memo back to the node.

You could be in the Node Explorer, reflecting on the relation between this (highlighted) node and others, or in the Node Browser, reviewing text coded at the node.

Link a new memo to a node

- Click on the DocLinks icon 🗏 on the toolbar of the Explorer or the Browser. NVivo will make a top-level DocLink—a node memo is linked to the node as a whole, rather than to one specific segment of text coded at the node.

- Choose to Link a New Memo. A blank document named [Node Title] - Memo will open in a Document Browser, ready for you to record your thoughts.

While reviewing the text at the node, you can swap back and forth between the Document Browser displaying the memo and the Node Browser displaying the node as you work through a read-think-record cycle. Click on any exposed part of the Browser you wish to go to (preferably the Title Bar at top or Status Bar at bottom, to avoid changing cursor positions)—NVivo will have arranged them in an overlapping fashion so that you can always see some part of the other Browser. Or minimize the Browser for the memo and bring it up each time you have further thoughts about the node. Or, given that the memo is automatically named for the node, simply identify and select it from the document list. If needed, text can be copied from the Node Browser to the Document Browser.

The node and its memo both "know" they are linked. If you go to either, and click on the link icon for the other on the toolbar (or request using the context menu) the resulting dialogue will show the node(s) or document(s) linked at the top level. For example, to access the linked node while browsing the memo:

- Click on the NodeLink icon in the browser's toolbar or choose NodeLinks from the right mouse button menu.
- Click on Show top-level NodeLinks.
- Select the linked node, and click on Browse. The text of the node will be opened in a Node Browser window.

Creating node links

Coding and its review can lead to linking data in different ways. Often you want to link not with a document, but with all the data you have on a particular topic. Linking a node to a specific position in your text allows fast access to everything coded at that node, taking you from text you are writing or reviewing directly to nodes being discussed. They can be particularly useful in your Project Journal when you are recording thoughts generated by a review of coding, as you can visit this evidence while you ponder the usefulness of the category.

The node link allows you to jump not only from a specific comment to all the text coded on that issue or topic, but also to the context of that text. So linking with a node provides a direct path to everything on a topic, and an indirect path to other related documents, and from there to the nodes that code them. Using such links, you can build up a web of evidence and growing understanding about a topic or issue for your analysis.

Link document text to a node

- In the Document Browser, click at the text to be linked so that your cursor is showing as an insertion point.

- Click on the NodeLinks icon in the toolbar at the top of the Document Browser.

- In the NodeLinks dialogue, double-click on Free or Trees to expand the list. Highlight the node you want to link, then click on the arrow to move that node to the right pane, under Nodes linked. Note you could link more than one node here, if you wished.

- Choose to Browse Node at this point if you wish, or simply Close the dialogue.

- The NodeLink symbol will appear in your text to indicate a node link exists. Click on the node link symbol, right mouse click, and from the context menu immediately access the linked node and review its text.

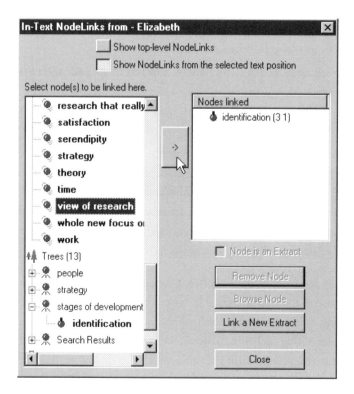

Note that this link, like any other data link, will persist in coded text. If you code that passage and meet it in a Node Browser, you will still be taken to that node. If you move the node, NVivo will adjust and maintain the link.

Record in the Journal what was learned from your examination and/or comparison of codes carried out earlier. (Don't forget to use a heading, and to date your work!) As you refer to each of the nodes being discussed, place a link to that node, so that it can be easily accessed. By the time those thoughts are reviewed later in the project, the node(s) may have changed "shape"—if so, that will be of interest in itself.

Extract Nodes

Extract Nodes are a special kind of NodeLink. They link to just the segment or quotation you want to jump to, rather than to a whole document or all the text coded at a node. Extract nodes provide an alternative to cutting and pasting text from the document or node you are writing about. Create the hyperlink, then record your reflections on that text. A click of the mouse will then retrieve the segment when you review earlier thoughts. Extracts are particularly useful in writing memos or recording a Project Journal, when you wish to keep close to the data.

Create an extract node

D.I.Y.

- In a document (e.g. your Project Journal) find a place where the text would be strengthened by a hyperlink to an extract from a document you are writing about. Place your cursor there.

- Click on the NodeLink icon in the Browser's toolbar. The NodeLinks dialogue appears. Choose to Link a New Extract.

- From the Choose Document box, select the document you wish to code the extract from. It will now open in a Document Browser with the new Extract Node created and showing in the Speed Coding slot.

- Highlight the passage you wish to have as a linked extract, and click Code. The passage is now coded at the new Extract Node.

- Close the Browser. In the NodeLinks dialogue, the Extract Node now appears under Nodes linked. Click Close to return to the original document (your memo or Journal), and see the NodeLink icon now showing in the text.

To view the extract, click on the NodeLink symbol, right mouse click, and from the context menu immediately access the linked node and browse its text. The extract appears in a normal Node Browser, so as with any coded text you can show wider context, recode, or jump to the extract in the original document.

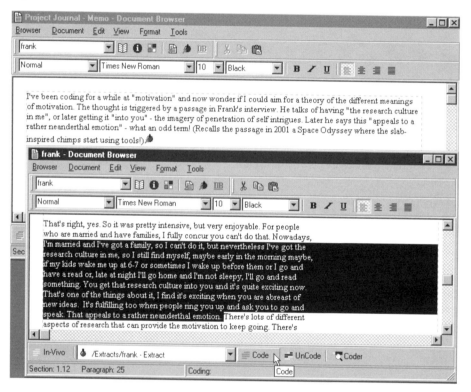

These features make Extracts valuable in preliminary exploration, memoing and reporting. The data on which your observations depend, or the vivid illustration that makes your point, can be immediately accessible via the NodeLink. Note that this link, like any other data link, will persist in coded text. If you meet it in a Node Browser, you will still be taken to that node.

Category development—focusing and extending

Many researchers, when they start working with their data, feel lost in the rich detail of it. As they try to capture that richness, "wallowing" in multiple codes, they may wonder how they're ever going to sort it all out. (It's perhaps a particular problem for those of us with a quantitative background, where we feel that every detail has to be "nailed down" or it will be lost forever.) It may be time to refocus on what the research question is—for the sanity of the researcher as well as for theory emergence!

If this is your problem, there are questions you need to be asking as you approach coding a passage that will assist you. What are the real issues here? With which people, or time periods, or sites, am I really concerned at the moment, out of all those that are mentioned in the segment of text that is in front of me? How is coding that detail going to help me understand the issues I'm concerned about, the questions I want to answer?

The tools for reshaping nodes, for discriminating and combining categories, used in conjunction perhaps with the search tool, allow the researcher to keep focused in the confidence that should something be "lurking", it can be revealed in due course. If new patterns are revealed, then the text can be recoded to reflect this (or may indeed be recategorized for you as the result of using the search tool).

Initially I had a tendency to code in detail the experiences people had and the people involved, for example, that research was presented as <u>exciting</u> and <u>interesting</u> by Elizabeth's <u>relatives</u> and was the source of dinner table discussions. Later I decided it was sufficient to note that Elizabeth's family background featured a strong research ethos. Later, my pool of data on research ethos may be reviewed, and/or viewed in relation to other categories like research career outcomes, using the Search Tool. That will be the time to see potential and perhaps surprising patterns for further exploration. Should those patterns involve specific categories of people, I can then code on to more specific nodes. Thus relying on the tools for searching and reshaping nodes saves a lot of time trying to pre-empt what might prove important.

Discriminating and combining categories

As a node is developed, it is often appropriate to relocate or reshape it, in the light of the new meanings, or new material coded there. In these processes you move "outside" the one node, to reflect on and revise its relations with other categories.

One way of moving outside is to "dimensionalize" a category, seeking and establishing new layers of meaning within it; perhaps as you see that it takes different shades or forms in different contexts. Or if it was created originally in what we have called "broad brush coding", you may now be seeing finer categories this data can be properly allocated to, or associated concepts that need to be tagged and further explored. What is happening now is that finer categories are "emerging" not from the data document but from the broader category.

The flip-side of this process is the recognition that fine categories you originally created actually mean the same thing. Early in the project you may have coded very finely until you were assured you weren't overlooking distinctions or dimensions that may later matter. Now the dust is settling and your confidence is building, you may wish to remove these picky distinctions. NVivo allows merging of nodes, without wasting any of the coding or memos they carry.

Code–on to finer categories

In Part 5 we introduced the important idea of coding-on. If, while reviewing the text at a node, you see that you have coded several different things at the one node, you can work from the Node Browser to code-on to finer categories (or indeed, totally different categories)—without needing to return to the Document Browser(s).

- Browse the text at the node. Decide on a way of splitting this into two (or more) subtly (or unsubtly!) different categories.

- Select a coded segment, or part of a segment that would fit better in a new or other existing category. Create the new node either by In-Vivo coding or typing the new title into the Speed Coding slot or the Coder.

- Code the selected text on to this new node.

- Then, if appropriate, remove the original coding by selecting the original node in the Speed Coding slot and clicking on Uncode while the text is still highlighted.

If the new categories are clearly subcategories of the original node, then it is best if the original node is moved to the Trees area, so the subcategories can be placed under it.

Merge two nodes into one

Merging nodes is carried out in the Node Explorer, as described in Part 5. Now that you have done more coding and established links at the nodes, you may need to consider your choices more carefully:

- Highlight the node you wish to move (the "source node"). From the context menu, select Cut.

- Highlight the node you wish to merge into (the "target node"). From the context menu, select Merge Node.

- Check the nodes and the selections in the resulting dialogue, before clicking OK. Your selections will reflect your reasons for doing this. If you leave coding selected, for example, the text now coded at the new combined node will retain coding at any other nodes it was already coded at. Do you want that? If you leave links selected, the text whose coding was merged will bring with it any links to annotations, documents or other nodes. (If unsure, retain all those links; they can be deleted later.)

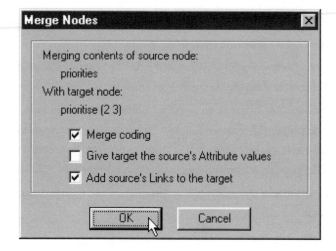

Reviewing categories and seeking associations

Do you have a hunch that two categories might be associated in some way, for example, that particular conditions or experiences are associated with each other or perhaps with certain outcomes? A Union search will place all the text for each category together for each document, while a Proximity search will show you the text from each category, providing both are present within a specified range of text (e.g. within the same document). Finding the Difference between the Union search results and the Proximity search results will then show where just one of the two categories was present. Examination of the text found by these different searches may not only provide information about the extent of the relationship between the experiences reported, but also give further clues about the nature of each of those experiences and whether they take on different meanings depending on whether the other is present or not.

Beginning with a Union search

D.I.Y.

* From the Project Pad, choose Search Project Database to open the Search Tool.

Run this search operation...

* Click on the search icon next to Boolean Search. A second dialogue will open.

* From the drop-down list next to Operator:, select Union (Or).

* Click on Choose Nodes to open the Choose Nodes dialogue. If you used this tool earlier, click on Remove All to clear the currently listed nodes.

* In the Choose Nodes dialogue select the first node you want to include in the search (say, a particular condition or experience). Click on Node in the centre panel to Add the node to the pane on the right of the dialogue. Repeat the process for the second node in your "query" (say, the possible outcome, or a possibly related experience). Click OK.

* The nodes you have selected will now show in the Boolean Search dialogue. Click OK.

in this scope...

* Click on Custom scope. Choose to Edit the list of Documents.

* In the Document Set Editor, choose All non-memo documents, or a particular set of data documents you wish to use for this search.

and handle results this way...

* Allow NVivo to save the results of the search at a new node, as a child of Search Results under Trees (that is, leave Use Custom Handling unchecked).

* Click Run Search.

* Choose to Browse Node. All text coded at either of the selected nodes will be shown.

Scan the text to see if there are occasions when the two nodes co-occur, and if so, whether there appears to be any significance in that, or how the text on those occasions differs from when they don't co-occur. You will find it helpful to create a Node Set for the nodes in the search, so you can view Selected Coding Stripes.

Using a Proximity search

- Open the Search Tool, and click on the icon next to Proximity Search.
- Choose to run a Co-occurrence (Near) search.
- Under Find where the text referenced by: Click on Choose Nodes and select the first of the nodes used in the Union search.
- Under ... is pairwise near text referenced by: click on Choose Nodes and select the second of the nodes used in the Union search.
- ...within this distance... Under Scope Documents, select in the same section level. Below that, identify the Section level as 0. (This means the search will locate the nodes if they co-occur anywhere in the same document.)
- ...and retrieve... Check Finds for the first item and Finds for the second item.
- Click OK to return to the Search Tool.
- Set the Custom Scope to All non-memo documents (or your preferred set of data, as used in the Union search).
- Click on Run Search, then on OK in the Search Completed dialogue.

View the resulting text using selected coding stripes.

Finding the difference

- In the Search Tool, choose Boolean Search, then Difference (Less) as the Operator.
- Under Find text referenced by any of these items... click on Choose Nodes and select the node resulting from the Union search (you will find this located under Search Results in the Trees area).
- Under ...but by none of these items select the node resulting from the Proximity search (/ Search Results/Co-occurrence).
- Click OK to return to the Search Tool, then click on Run Search.
- Again, view the resulting text using selected coding stripes.

And evaluate

It is now up to you to determine if there was any meaningful association between the categories you included in your search, and also whether either seemed to be expressed differently in documents where the other was absent.

There are many ways in which the results of using the Search Tool may assist in reconceptualization of your categories, or in contributing to emerging theory about the relationship between categories. If the answer to any of these questions was "yes", then there may be further work to be done either in coding-on, or in undertaking more searches—or perhaps you will hold on that until you have more data and re-check the patterns then. If so, a note in your Journal reminding you to do so is warranted. Indeed, a note is warranted in any case to record what was done and its outcome—even if there was no apparent result, to say just that!

Researchers 4 includes additional coded documents which will allow you to experiment with some of the suggested searches. You might check out combinations of enjoyment with intellectual stimulation, enjoyment with satisfaction, or look to see what kinds of background factors are associated with identification as a researcher. See if you can begin to generate some theory from the data—and send your fresh insights to Pat!

Modeling relationships

Theory emergence requires not only discovering and developing categories, but starting to locate them and explore their relationships. At this stage, researchers usually find they are starting to *construct* theory. NVivo provides for many different ways of establishing category relationships. How are categories occurring in the data? To answer this, the patterns of coding have to be searched, viewed and discussed. What relation do categories seem to have to each other, and how does this explain the data? To explore this, the researcher can write memos and draw and layer models. And how are categories logically related? To establish and investigate the logical ways categories belong together, nodes can be ordered in trees and shifted as their logical relations change. We conclude this Part with ideas for ways of mapping relationships in models, while in Part 7, we will focus on ways of establishing and cataloging categories in a logical index system.

Modeling offers a quite different way of seeing ideas from searching coding or creating a tree of nodes. Searches shows how codes are falling in patterns. A node tree shows the logical relations of nodes. A model provides an opportunity to sketch and think about *any* current, possible or potential relation of categories. In a model you may explore any ideas visually—they may be ideas about patterns that are emerging, ideas about logical relations, or ideas that are so far not showing in coding or logic.

NVivo's modeler is designed to be used to see how your picture changes when you move, hide or group ideas, without impacting on the project database. Models can be built up in layers to explore or demonstrate the impact of added items or item groups.

At this point you can simply add new items to your previous model, you can create a new model, or you can develop layers in your model. Use models to "toy" with particular relationships you are thinking about in the data, or try building a model which shows general trends from across the data so far considered.

Building layers in a model

D.I.Y.
- Identify a concept, node or document to show in your model, and bring it on to the screen. Select that item.
- From the right mouse button (context) menu, select Layer, and choose New.
- You will be asked: Please give the new layer a title. Type your title in the slot provided. Click OK.

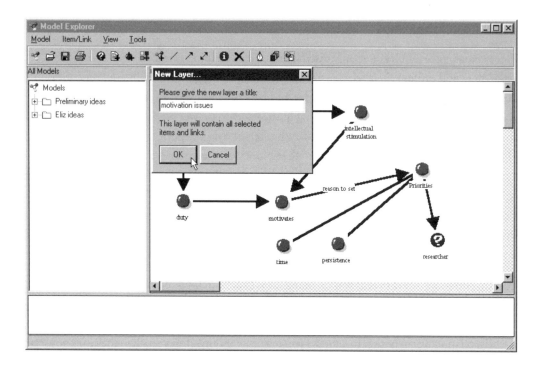

- From the View menu, select Layer Palette. The Layer Palette will show on the left of your screen.

- Click the checkbox for the new layer, rather than All. Anything you now add to your model will be added only to this layer (unless you later direct otherwise). Click on All while you add further nodes, and these will not show when you check to see only the new layer.

Working in the layer

Now "play" in the model with the various concepts, nodes and documents you have created, to convey the story you have found so far.

- Click on icons in the Modeler's toolbar to give you easy access to nodes or documents you wish to include in your model.

- Add in new concepts as necessary, using the New Item icon from the toolbar. Double click to label them, or label and change their appearance via Properties.

- Provide links to show relationships. Use the context menu to access Properties, so that you can name the selected link, or change its style.

- If you are unsure whether or not to include an item, check its contents: you can retrieve the text in a Browser by highlighting an item and selecting Browse/Code Node (or Document) from the context menu.

Build another layer

- Highlight an item (or multiple items) you wish to show in a new layer. Choose Layers, then New, from the context menu.

- Provide a name for the new layer. Note that it will contain all currently selected items.

- Click the checkbox for the new layer in the Layer Palette, and de-select any other or All layers. The new layer containing just the selected items will show on the right pane of the Modeler.

- Add further items to your new layer.

To use an item that already exists in the first layer, first extend the list of items in the model in the left pane of the Model Explorer (click on the + next to the name of the model). Select the item you want to add to your new layer. From the context menu, choose Layer, then the name of your new layer (so that it is ticked). The item will now show in your new layer. If you move its position, it will be moved (and links adjusted) in both layers of your model.

At any time you can elect to see any or all layers of your model together. This provides an alternative opportunity for copying the same item into a second layer (From the context menu, select Layer, and check against the desired layer). You can add any links between the two layers while All layers are showing.

You might not find it useful to create a layered model at this early stage. You can always create a series of separate models, on the way through. Any model can be added to another model. Browse the item to open it. These are tools to be used as best suits you and what you want to achieve. As ideas change, recall the ability to layer a model, viewing and reflecting on the growth of your theory through visual interpretations, or just disconnected views of the data. They may suddenly connect when you view all layers!

Pasting your model into a report in Word

When you are satisfied with your new model:

- From the Model menu, choose Export Diagram to Clipboard.

- Open a document in Word.

- Paste your diagram then save the document.

    Note that you could choose to paste the diagram into Powerpoint or any other program capable of displaying a picture.

If your purpose in pasting the model is to link it to your Journal, then save the Word document in the specially provided folder for your Project—C:\QSR Projects\[your project]\All Users\External DataBites); this helps keep track of the location of the DataBites when you move a project.

Linking a model to a document

A final task is appropriate after this excursion in theory emergence. Much of what has happened during this Part should doubtless be recorded in the Project Journal. The model should go there too!

Perhaps you wish to write about the ways you have discovered, explored and developed categories, and the ways you examined patterns of coding. If a model you have just drawn is pertinent to this account, it is easy to include a link to the model from any document in NVivo. This can be done by placing an External DataBite.

Use an External DataBite to link to a model

- Open your Project Journal to record thoughts that developed while creating your model.

- Use a DataBite to link those comments to the Word document with the diagram you exported from the Modeler.

Taking Stock

One of the most exciting discoveries of qualitative research is that theory does emerge if the researcher actively seeks it in working with the data and the categories. At the end of this Part, our hope is that most readers will have no problem finding and developing categories, and seeing ways to start exploring their relationships. The most likely problem is that the emergence of categories is becoming somewhat alarming! Anselm Strauss remarked cheerfully to one of us years ago, "We generate categories like God creates raindrops!" To do that without control will mean you just get wet. So at this stage the management of categories is likely to become a high priority, if the researcher is to retain the ability to hold and explore all the ideas emerging and to use them consistently and efficiently. Happily, and not entirely by coincidence, managing categories is also a high priority for theory construction. It is to that task that we turn now.

In the context of the earlier exploratory Parts, the tools for managing nodes in hierarchical trees are just one way of shaping data. You will rapidly find however that this is a special way. NVivo does not require that you order nodes, but nodes almost always have a logical relation, and sometimes a very strong one. A logical organization of the nodes serves to clarify the extent and focus of the project, and the emerging structure of the ideas being generated or tested through the project. It allows you to find nodes easily and use them reliably. As ideas change, grow or become more refined, a tree structure for holding those ideas can reflect those changes. As with the shaping tools in the earlier Parts, the tools for ordering concepts are designed to be used constantly and in context of coding, memoing, reflecting, browsing, and editing. This Part is designed to help ensure that you get the structure of your concepts and categories into the kind of order that will allow you to work effectively with your data. Many of its tools are, by now, familiar—yet there are new ways of using them to explore, clarify and refine, as you move toward the goal of fresh insight and new understanding.

Thinking trees

The idea of placing nodes in trees was introduced earlier primarily as a way of setting out subcategories or dimensions of a concept, with trees being created and used on a relatively *ad hoc* basis. As these develop, most researchers wish to organize nodes systematically into conceptual trees, or a hierarchical index system, much as a library catalogues its books. In creating trees and managing them, you clarify your ideas about what goes with what, see missing categories, and solidify categories that overlap. Thus they will be informed by, and in turn will inform the analytical and theory building processes of the researcher.

It may be that in your project, much of the work covered in this Part is already done. It is, however, our experience that far too often researchers struggle on, encumbered by a confused or cluttered index system that inhibits rather than enhances their analysis. Much can be seen about a project simply by reviewing its index system. Usually, a "healthy" well-conceptualized and well-organized index system, or tree structure, is a sign of a project that is progressing well toward a conclusion.

All qualitative methods—and all human thinking!—involve abstracting from the particular to the general. The ability to see a particular concept (e.g. "academic family") as one of a grouping ("family background") helps the researcher manage concepts and think more abstractly. (Now we can wonder how different family backgrounds pattern experience.) If this concept ordering process is new to you, try adding a further question to the coding questions in Part 4: now asking not just, "Why am I interested in *that*?" but, "What is this a *sort of*?" Academic family is a *sort of* family background.

Sorting nodes

A tree structure, like any catalogue, is a logical organization of nodes, not a model of what you think you are finding out from your data. Thus each node has a place with other concepts of that sort. Treat the trees as expressing where each concept logically *fits*: use the search processes to ask questions about the *relations* between concepts. For example, if you were coding who takes responsibility for certain tasks, you would code the person and the task in separate trees. Conceptually, the person is a "who", and the task is a "what". The temptation is to use trees as a shortcut to represent relationships between categories, so that, for example, one might create a node called "worry about future income", perhaps with subcategories of father and/or mother. But father also worries about his children's behaviour, and the future of the education system. And teachers also worry about the future of the education system, or the behaviour of children in it, while the politicians are confident that the education system is "in good shape" and blame parents for the poor behaviour of their children. If the person is always a subcategory of the issue, the result is a proliferation of nodes. It also makes for an inability to find a node for coding, or to find out who worried about what, or what fathers thought more generally, or how anyone viewed children's behaviour.

Instead, organize the who, what and how in separate trees, and if particular text is about many of these, code it many times (one for each of the who, what and how). Use the search tool to discover who does what how, under which circumstances. Assumptions about relationships between categories are then a matter of investigation, not an artefact of the coding system.

There are several steps to this process of creating some conceptual order in a coding system. The first critical step is a thinking-sorting process, to decide how your nodes might be arranged. Then nodes are shifted so their order reflects conceptual relationships. Normally, these steps are engaged in several cycles. But first, it would be helpful to start by simply printing a list of the nodes you have already created. Periodically throughout your project, you will want to print a list of nodes to assess how ideas are growing, what's missing, where there are duplications and whether they are forming conceptual groups. As your nodes are moved into Trees, the list of nodes becomes a practical tool to assist comprehensive and speedy coding.

Listing nodes

*   From the Nodes menu at the top of the Project Pad, choose List all Nodes, asking for Titles and Addresses Only.

NVivo will create a report listing all nodes—first the Free Nodes, then Trees, with the trees in numeric sequence based on their node addresses. This can be edited (e.g. to place some blank lines between Trees, or to bold the parent nodes), saved and/or printed.

Grouping nodes

*   Look carefully at your list of nodes, and think about them in terms of conceptual groupings. Are there a few that are sorts of a more general concept? Sometimes, those general groups will be obvious from the research design: Ask "What am I asking?" and see what groups of categories the answer contains. If it is a study of how different people, at different sites, act in different ways; those are three sorts of categories. Sometimes the groups appear during the sorting of categories emerging from the data. There may be nodes for different experiences or interpretations, such as different images of research, and grouping these becomes sensible as their variety is established.

- Sketch out the groups you are coming up with on a piece of paper, or, if you want to work in NVivo, draw them in the modeler. Try to see where each Free Node might fit (and any Tree Nodes you might already have). If there are some nodes "left over", don't worry—they can stay as Free Nodes for the time being (or forever!).

  Most projects end up with around 10 major groupings, or trees—sometimes less and rarely much more.

- In the process of deciding on how to combine or sort your nodes, regularly browse their content, jumping from one to another, checking back to documents to see why the text that you "knew" was about something doesn't seem to be coded there, and so on. This adds another way of seeing your text anew. Additionally, thinking about possible ways of organizing the structure of your knowledge about your data prompts rethinking about what you are looking for in that data—about the goals of your project. The questions you are seeking to answer will, of course, have a major impact on how your coding is organized.

Review (in the Node Explorer) the list of nodes to be found in **Researchers** 4. Apart from those constructed in the process of doing searches (which you may have added to when working through Part 6!) you will find that there are around 30 Free Nodes and 35 nodes that are placed in beginning Trees. Start scribbling some headings for trees down the side of a page of paper, and sketch in where you think various nodes would fit. Ask, "Why am I interested in that?" or, "What is this a sort of?" if you're stalling on where to place a node, although there will be some that strongly resist classification.

Some nodes obviously go together. Deal with the easy ones first, to get some sense of achievement here: People and Actions are two good places to start. You'll probably need to sketch them out in branching format on a fresh piece of paper after a bit because you will have created an unreadable mess. There will be some you are moving from tree to tree, because you can't quite work out where they fit. I initially found motivation, duty and goals to be particularly problematic in the Researchers project, for example, yet some of these are quite critical nodes for this project. Remember that your coding system is flexible and ever changing: you can keep thinking about a concept, move it as your thinking changes, or recode or code-on from that concept into other or finer categories.

From "sorts" to structure

The "emergence" of a conceptual shape to the project is an exciting stage. You created Free Nodes up out of the data. Now you are creating a more abstract framework up out of those early categories. Working up from the particular to the general requires new nodes for the higher level, or "parent" nodes—some also referred to as "top-level" nodes, to indicate their tree position. Earlier, generally, you created nodes while coding, but not all nodes will have coding. Some now serve, rather, as "coat hangers" for ordering other nodes.

Creating Tree Nodes

You can create nodes without coding in the Node Explorer or the Coder, placing the node where you want it—indeed, you have probably already done so. These are convenient methods if you are creating an occasional node; but a third method, working in the Create Nodes dialogue, is faster if you have several nodes to create.

As you create Tree Nodes, each is automatically assigned a number. Every node is identified by a node address, a numeric code for where it is located within the index system. Addresses appear in the right pane of the Node Explorer, in the status bar at the bottom of the Node Explorer when you select a node, and the Properties box. Most usefully, they are included in a list of nodes (as seen above). Whereas in NUD*IST 4 knowing the node address was necessary for adding coding, in NVivo you can manage quite well without ever thinking about node addresses, but they can make coding faster and are also a useful way of seeing order in your coding system.

Some trees may need branches before they can take specific nodes. For example, if nodes are in groups for setting, period of time, and the prevailing atmosphere, these could be placed as three branches of a <u>context</u> tree. Specific settings or times or atmospheres are then coded at sub-nodes under these branches.

Create tree nodes

D.I.Y.

- Working in the Node Explorer or the Coder, use the very intuitive method of selecting Trees, or the node at which you want to create a branch, and from the right mouse context menu selecting Create.

Alternatively

- From the Project Pad, select Make a Project Node, or from the Nodes menu at the top of the Project Pad, choose Create Nodes.

- Click on the Trees tab. (Free Nodes can also be created this way.) Any Tree Nodes you have created already will show in the left pane of the dialogue.

- Click in the Title slot on the right side of the dialogue, and type in a new tree node title. Press Enter on your keyboard (or click Create with the mouse). The node will be created.

- Type the next title (no need to click in the slot again), and Enter.

- Type and Enter until you have all the parent (top-level) nodes you want.

Create "children" of a Tree node

- In the left pane of the Create Nodes dialogue, double-click on the Tree Node for which you wish to create sub categories ("children"). Its title appears in the slot above (immediately under Tree Nodes:).

- Click in the Title slot on the right side of the dialogue, and type in a title for the first "child" node. Make sure the Address slot (under the title slot) is set at 1. Press Enter.

- Now, as before, type in a title followed by pressing Enter for as many times as you need to create all nodes at this level (rarely more than 2-4). If the node you want already exists as a Free Node, then don't create it here—it can be moved directly across from the Free Nodes area, with its coding references (text stored there) intact (see below).

Shifting Free Nodes into Trees

You have already discovered that nodes can be Cut or Copied and Pasted in NVivo, using either the Node Explorer or the Coder. The context menu on the right mouse button makes these very accessible tools also. Working in the Coder or using the context menu is fine if you want to shift just one or two while you are working on a document or node, but the best place to move nodes for the current task will be in the Node Explorer. Here you can easily extend your view of all your trees, and multiple options are offered for moving, reshaping and restructuring nodes. These options will now be presented in detail (including a brief repetition of the basic ones presented in Part 5) so you have before you the full set of choices available. It then becomes a matter of choosing the method that suits your personal style for the specific task in hand!

Remember there is no requirement that all Free Nodes be moved into Trees. It is likely that some Free Nodes will never be located under a more generic category. You may not be sure whether you want to keep that node, or perhaps it is an "outlier", a maverick idea that will continue outside the more orderly system. For some methodologies, these unattached categories may be the crucial theoretical sparks that will inform the ultimate analysis. So Free Nodes are special. Move them into Trees only when this ordering does them justice.

You might be about to do something drastic. How long since you saved the project? Save now and also Save Project As with a different name (*before* embarking on a reorganization!). You can always return to the backup if you make a move you regret later!

When you are moving your nodes, have beside you a sketch of how you wish to organize them. A separate checklist of Free Nodes (to mark off when they have been moved) may also be helpful. But before you start on moving, it is useful to understand more fully the variety of ways in which the Node Explorer can be put to work.

Node Explorer revisited

- Click once on Free (or Trees) in the left hand pane of the Node Explorer. All Free (Tree) Nodes appear in the right hand pane, along with information about how many passages they code, and when they were created and last modified. For Tree Nodes, the specific tree address is given as additional information.

- Double-click on Free (or Trees) in the left pane. It will expand to show any Free (Tree) Nodes. They will also be listed on the right pane (as before). In the list on the left side, those which have coding at them will be shown in bold.

- Note the different icons: Tree Nodes with children have "legs" hanging from their blue icons (in both left and right panes). Those with children also have a + next to them (in the left pane) to indicate that they can be expanded further.

- Click once on a Tree Node with children. The children will show in the right pane of the Node Explorer. Double-click and the Tree will be expanded in the left pane.

- Click on any node to see its coding status and description (lower right pane).

The two sides of the Node Explorer allow different things to be done to nodes.

In the left pane:

- Single click on a highlighted node title to edit its title.

- Click on any node title to select it, then on Browse to open it in a Node Browser.

In the right pane:

- Double click on any node title to open the Node Browser for that node (but this will expand the source list in the left pane—if it wasn't already—leaving the right pane blank).

- Click on any node title to select it, then click on Browse, to open the Node Browser for that node without altering the list in either pane. (This is very useful when you want to check the contents of a Free Node while you have the trees showing in the left pane).

- Select multiple nodes using Ctrl-click (e.g. if you want to move a number of nodes to the same location, or to delete multiple nodes).

In either pane:

- Select any node and click on the appropriate toolbar icon (or choose from the context menu) to access its Properties, Attributes, DocLinks or NodeLinks.

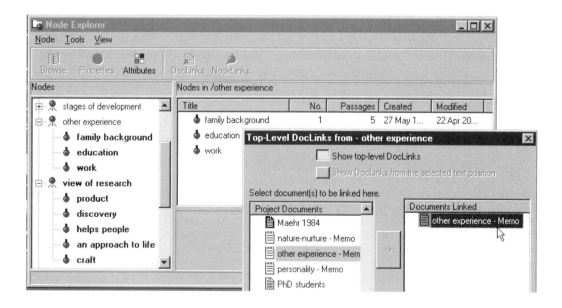

Moving Free Nodes to Trees using drag-and-drop

To "drag" a node, like text in a word processor, involves selecting the node using the left mouse button, then clicking on the selected node and moving the mouse while continuing to hold down the left mouse button, until the destination is reached.

- Expand or extend the Node Explorer (drag the bottom right corner down) so that it shows more nodes at one time.

- In the left pane, expand the Trees to show the top level nodes, and any main branches. Click once on Free, so the Free Nodes show in the right pane.

- Drag a Free Node from the right pane to the required tree (or branch) in the left pane. It will be attached to that tree or branch as a child node.

- If several nodes are to become children in the same tree, multiple select them (use Ctrl-click) and drag them together to that tree.

 When you drag a Free Node to a Tree, it is copied rather than moved (rather like moving a file from one disk to another). You should then delete it from the Free Node list (see below for how), to avoid later confusion.

Moving nodes from tree to tree with drag-and-drop

- Drag from the right pane to the left, or drag within the left pane—whichever is more convenient. (This will depend on how much of the tree structure you can see in the left pane).

If you drag a node from one tree to another, it is moved rather than copied and therefore does not need to be deleted.

 Sibling nodes can be rearranged by changing the nodes' addresses via the Node Properties dialogue.

Delete excess copies of nodes

- Highlight the node(s) you wish to delete (e.g. copies of Free Nodes you have just moved into a tree).

- From the context menu, select Delete Node. Confirm that you wish to delete the specific nodes you had selected—this is a useful safety check and it is worth paying attention to what is listed for deletion (can you hear the voice of experience speaking here?!).

Moving nodes using Cut and Paste

Cut and Paste is the method we recommended initially (in Part 5) if you needed to move a node. The advantage of this method is twofold: if you cut a node then paste it, you will not have to backtrack to delete it, and, you can paste the node more than once. Thus, if a Free Node comprises two separate concepts, you can paste it into two trees and develop both copies in directions appropriate to that tree. A Free Node remains on your clipboard no matter how many times you paste it, until you cut or copy another node. A further advantage of using Cut and Paste is its precision. Drag and drop must be used with caution, since it is easy to "drop" a node in the wrong place. Cut and Paste is recommended for the nervous researcher, Copy and Paste is great for the excessively nervous!

Combining and splitting nodes

By now you should also be already familiar with merging two nodes. Merging is a strong way of solidifying a node system—without losing any coding work. As with cutting and pasting, where the original node encompasses two meanings, you may need to merge it in two places, or paste it to one and merge with another. On some rare occasions it may be necessary to recode its contents into more than one place, using the same techniques as for coding-on, i.e. to code from the Node Browser into new or other existing nodes.

 Do not merge coding in this way unless you are sure: it is very difficult to undo the merge (even if you have copied the source node) because some text may have been coded at both nodes, while other text will have been coded at just one or the other.

Just checking!

Now that you have shifted all those nodes around, print out a fresh list of your nodes (Nodes menu, List all Nodes).

This will allow you to check that everything has ended up where you wanted it to be. More importantly, it will give you an overview of the conceptual shape of your coding system.

Create top-level Tree Nodes as needed for the plan you have developed from the nodes in the **Researchers** 4 database. Then move Free Nodes in under them. Some will need to be moved to or merged with nodes under trees that have been already created—and maybe also preserved for attaching or merging in a second place.

When you've completed as much moving as you are happy with, you might like to see what I ended up doing. The restructured tree is there for you to see in **Researchers** 5. You will find some of the thinking behind it recorded in the Project Journal. While I did the main changes over a morning, I kept "tweaking" it every time I worked with a new document or reviewed data.

Rearranging an index tree

Most of us need to rearrange trees at some stage (read of Pat's experience below!). The most common challenge is to tidy multiple repetitions of a particular group of nodes. In the example shown, from a study of workplace communication, the categories of people doing it may be repeated as subnodes of each type of communication. For just three sorts of communication, with four categories of staff, there are already 16 nodes. As the study progresses, the nodes will proliferate. But more importantly, the study is not keeping like concepts together (there is no one node, for example, where we can see everything the manager is doing). Unlike concepts are combined, and this will limit our ability to develop concepts. For example, subnodes of formal communication can't be developed as we see different ways of formally communicating.

Clearly the project needs two trees, one for staff categories and one for modes of communication.

Compare the Explorers below. Even at this early stage there is evident advantage in the simpler system—only 9 nodes, rather than 16, and the trees clarify what the project is about—patterns of communication by staff category.

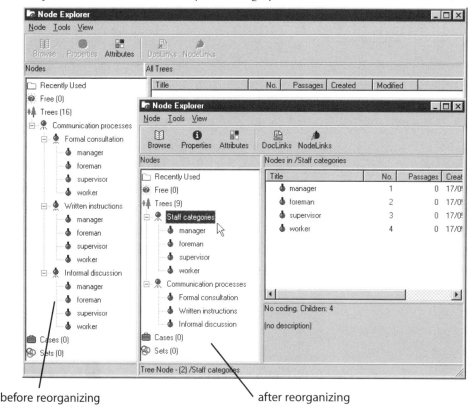

before reorganizing

after reorganizing

Transformation of this index system took three simple steps.

1. First, the nodes that were at the top level (Communication processes) are given all coding that was previously at the subnodes (so Formal consultation now codes everything previously coded at the staff member doing it, and so on). This requires a Union search. Now the Communication processes nodes, with all their coding, can be placed in their own tree.

2. Then all coding that was previously at each lot of duplicated nodes (those for Staff categories) is merged (so one node now codes everything previously coded at three nodes, for example, Manager). One tree is made for Staff categories.

3. All you have to do is delete the original nodes (having carefully checked you relocated the coding!)

The tools for this transformation are already familiar—gather coding at several nodes by Boolean Union search, copy, paste and merge nodes. The result is a clear framework for the study, and a change in your coding. If text is about the manager's style of formal consultation, it is coded twice. You can now easily find all that you have about that particular communication style, or all communication by the manager, and if you want to know how formal consultation was used by the manager, a Boolean Intersect search will quickly tell you.

D.I.Y.

1.   Collect all the text "below" a parent node

*   Choose to Search the Project Database and then to conduct a Boolean (Union) search (as you have done several times before, by now).

*   In the Choose Nodes dialogue, highlight the "parent" node for which you wish to gather coding at the "children" (and "grandchildren" if there are any), e.g. Formal consultation, in the example above. Click to Add the whole Subtree to the right pane of the dialogue, then OK to have those nodes show in the search dialogue.

*   Ensure that All Documents is showing as the scope for the search, then click on Run Search.

*   From the Search Completed dialogue, check Show Node in Explorer and uncheck Browse Node. The node will be shown, highlighted, in the Node Explorer. This new node now codes everything that was coded at the subnodes you specified. Note the text references have been *copied* from the original nodes (which are unchanged).

*   Click once on the highlighted node, and edit its title. You can use the intended name, e.g. Formal consultation, as it is not a sibling of the original).

- Create the required parent for the new node. (Call it something slightly different, e.g. Communication Styles, since you have not yet deleted the earlier tree.) Cut the node you made by the union search, pasting it under the new parent. Your new tree is begun.

- Repeat this process for each of the nodes to be brought into this tree.

2. Combine all the text of repeated nodes

- **Create** and title a parent node for the next new tree (Staff Categories). Copy the first of each repeated node (e.g. Manager) and Paste under the new parent.

- Copy the next repeated node and Merge with the one you just pasted. Repeat for as many repeated nodes as there are, to combine coding of all of them into one. (*If there are many repeats of each child node*, use a Union (Boolean) search to combine the text for all reports, in one step.)

3. A final tidy-up

- In the Node Explorer, click on each of the new nodes in your Tree and just check that the coding status (lower right pane) appears to be "about right", given the data you have now gathered together.

- Now select and Delete each of the original trees, branches or nodes that have been collected and relocated into two separate places (if you work in the right pane of the Node Explorer, you can use Ctrl-Click to multiple select them).

Be careful you don't include your new tree in the list for deletion, or, if you are deleting whole branches, that there aren't other nodes still buried within them that you want to retain! Note the method used above is the safe one, copying nodes rather than cutting them. For the brave, cut and merge will be faster—but back up first!!

When I initially started working with some data about what motivated researchers (in my first attempt to use NUD*IST—version 2!) I created a node called motivation and then created a series of nodes under that of things that had the effect of motivating academics to do research. That was fine until I began wondering what to do with these "things" if they were talked about, but in a different way—perhaps as part of the researcher's developmental experience, or simply as an outcome of their work, or even as a limitation. And so they reappeared in trees for development, and/or experience, and so on—and unfortunately not in neat repetitions. After some period of struggling with this cumbersome system, application of a flash of insight saw what had become a four page list reduced to one: have a tree for <u>impact</u> (stimulate, develop, maintain, reinforce, limit), with separate trees for the things that had an impact, such as people, events, activities; and others for the contexts that moderated those things and for the way people felt or otherwise responded. For any interesting segment of text, I would then code at as many of these as were relevant, and always think about applying a code for impact. The difficulty I had on the way was that re-organization of the existing nodes was complicated by their varied organisation and usage, and coupled with a sense that a lot of what was in the data had been missed because of the way I had been coding it, this led to my scrapping my first coding (and its attempted reorganization) and starting again. We're hoping you can avoid a need for such drastic action with our strategies for "early prevention"!

Using structure

At this stage it is important to ask—and keep asking—why you are making these nodes, and shaping them thus. Just as coding can become a ritualistic process, so node creation and ordering can become an end in itself. If this happens, the software is not being used to its full, and your project may come to a dead stop! Is the shape, or order, your nodes are taking going to assist you to explore and answer questions raised in and by your data?

Using trees while coding

Even before you launch into searching questions, well organized trees provide a useful tool for ensuring the thoroughness of your coding, as you are doing it. You've stopped to code a passage because an interesting issue has been raised there. Capture that, but before you leave the passage, run an eye over your tree structure as a quick visual prompt to see if there are other nodes that are relevant. Should you also note (code) who the key players are, what the context is, how people felt or otherwise responded? Do you need reminding about trees in which you want to routinely code all otherwise coded text in order to capture a key variable (maybe a contextual variable, maybe an outcome)? Making sure that the text is coded at nodes across all relevant trees will allow searches for answers to questions to be much more effective and complete.

Working with a printed list of nodes beside you is helpful for this kind of checking when coding. Before printing the list, add some visual clues to clarify the tree structure. For example, you might insert a blank line or two between each tree or remove the tab in front of the top-level node for each tree and/or make it bold.

Be prepared, of course, to add to and delete from the nodes in your list as you do further coding, and after a while, to regenerate and reprint the list. Don't expect it will ever become a fixture, even after the major sorting effort you have just undertaken!

 Having nodes in trees and working with a printed list beside you also makes for easier, faster coding, as will be seen in Part 8.

Using trees to explore with searches

Having ordered and coded in this way allows you to ask exploratory and comparative questions with ease. For example, one might ask: "What issues arise in this context?" and then perhaps, for an issue that appears interesting in that context: "How does this issue look in other, different contexts?" These kinds of questions can be investigated using the Boolean search operator Matrix Intersection with the relevant nodes.

An intersection of nodes occurs where they code the same text, thus a request to NVivo to find the intersection of two nodes will result in NVivo finding all the text that is coded at (or in technical terms, referenced by) both of those nodes. Anything coded at just one or the other, or at neither, will be ignored. A matrix intersection simply does this for several subcategories of a node (or several listed nodes) in parallel: the same result could be obtained by running a separate intersection search for each pair, but it would take much longer to do. The further advantage of running the searches in parallel and building a matrix is that it enhances the sense of what is being done here—that you are wanting to examine the patterning of and perhaps draw comparisons between elements of a concept when it is viewed in relation to something else.

You *could* run a matrix intersection search where you cross tabulate all issues (say) by all contexts, to produce a full table with a number of rows and columns and many cells. This can be useful for getting an overview of the pattern of distribution of what issues arise in what contexts, but for the purpose outlined here is likely to provide information overload and lead to some confusion about what is being searched for. It is better in this situation to make meaningful comparisons a step at a time, thinking about the implications of the first step before taking the second.

Tip

It is a statistical convention to use columns for "independent variables" and rows for "dependent variables" in cross tabulations. While there is no demand to maintain this convention (and such terms may be totally inappropriate to the data you are working with), for those of us with such training, it makes sense to follow the convention wherever it does seem appropriate.

D.I.Y.

Find (and compare) the issues that arise in a particular context

- Choose to Search the Project Database. In the Search Tool, choose to run a Boolean search.

- In the Boolean Search dialogue, from the slot next to Operator: select Matrix Intersection as the specific search you want to run.

- Under Find text referenced by each of these items… select to Choose Nodes. The node(s) you select for this first slot will define the row(s) of your matrix. Highlight [Issues] in your list of nodes and choose to Add > Children. The list of specific issues you have created will be listed on the right.

- Under …pairwise with each of these items, again Choose Nodes, this time choosing just the specific [context] you wish to explore. Node(s) chosen in this pane define the column(s) of your matrix.

- Click OK to return to the Search Tool, and specify the scope for your search.

- Run Search, and click OK in the Search Completed dialogue to be taken to a view of the Matrix results. If you followed the choice of nodes suggested, this will be presented as a single column (one context) containing multiple rows of data (one row for each of the selected issues).

- In the slot next to Display: choose a form of display for your results (probably Number of documents coded is most useful). The level of shading, along with the number shown will indicate how much coding there is in any cell of the matrix display. This will give you some sense of the distribution of (in the example here) issues that arise in this particular context.

- Choose a cell of interest (a particular issue), and from the context (right mouse) menu select Browse/Code Node. A Node Browser will open to show just the text that was coded at those two nodes, that is, for both that issue and that context.

- Browse as many cells as are of interest. If you want to print the results, a coding report can be made for any cell (if you do so, type under the node address the titles of the nodes that were intersected to produce that result, before printing or saving it).

Compare an issue across contexts

Do you want to follow up on the previous search by taking a particular issue of interest and comparing its "shape" in different contexts. The procedure is almost identical to that outlined above.

- Run a Matrix Intersection search, as before, but this time select just the one issue node, and choose to find the text where it intersects with each of the context nodes. The result will be a table running across rather than down.

- Browse each cell of the matrix to see whether this issue takes different forms, depending on the context in which it arises.

That may be sufficient for your needs. Perhaps, however, in your reading of the text, you will become aware of specific factors operating in those contexts which need further examination or elaboration (with further searches, or additional coding and searching).

Open **Researchers 5** (if it isn't already). Investigate the kinds of emotional experiences that were reported by the interviewees when talking about the time they were becoming researchers (Matrix Intersection, children of \Experiences of research\emotional, paired with: \Stages of development\Becoming a researcher). Then take one or more of these emotions and compare the way it is recorded there with the way it is recorded in the context of being a researcher. Does the researcher's emotional experience change as they develop?

Taking stock

Research approaches use concept ordering in different ways. For some researchers, it is essential to manage all concepts in efficient index systems. For others, the ordering of concepts will be critical in identification of core categories and development of their dimensions. Projects that have short time-lines and aim at descriptive reports rather than theory construction are less likely to require very careful concept management than projects which over time aim to develop theories and validate them.

Thus the effort you spend on concept ordering will depend on your method and your goals. But no matter how important this is (indeed, perhaps particularly when it is very important) it should not become either ritualistic or onerous. Locating of nodes happens when you think about coding (What is it about and where does *that* go?). Reorganizing of nodes happens whenever you see a node that would fit better elsewhere, and this happens very frequently.

Many things are happening at once, the concepts emerging and being tested, the data building up and the ideas accruing in annotations and memos. It is easy to delay locating nodes in the heat of the chase for meaning and understanding. Understanding however will require rigorous exploration and interrogation of just these concepts, and their orderly management will help you avoid partial or arbitrary reliance on just some concepts, or failure to see their uneven association. So the way to avoid wasting time is not to delay locating and ordering concepts, rather to build it into the process of thinking aloud about the data. Every time you pick up an idea, put it somewhere thoughtfully.

Once the tools are familiar, it is quicker to move the node than to worry about it, or make a note that later you should do so. When you move it, the coding and memo and attributes are not lost. So the profit is a constantly changing and synthesizing picture of the project and its ideas, and the price is seconds of time.

Part 8 is about saving more time by automating clerical work, so time can be better spent on the more creative work of interpretation.

Part 8: Moving faster

Your project is now taking shape. Having worked through the first few documents in some detail, you are probably gathering analytical insights. If the data are fairly homogeneous, by the time you have coded around six documents, you are likely to find the rate of expansion of your nodes is lessening. Conceptual shifts can occur at any time, but generally speaking it is unlikely that you will undertake another major reorganization of your index system in the way described in Part 7. Now you will want to pursue those ideas through more documents, whilst remaining open to new understanding and insights from any additional data. At this stage you will be helped by tools that automate clerical work, so you can concentrate on interpretive work. In this part, we deal with ways of speeding up document import, coding, attribute import and handling of sets and cases.

"Batching in" multiple documents

It is possible in NVivo to import multiple documents at the same time, so long as their title and description paragraphs are set up on a similar basis. If you now have another four or five documents ready (for most projects, this is much better than 40 or 50!) you might want to import them all at once. Then you can move to a rhythm of coding/ memoing/ annotating/ linking them, with additional techniques to assist in working through.

If "batching" documents in multiples has never occurred to you, please don't feel you should be doing it! This is a good instance of the crucial rule that you should never feel required to do something because your software can. Many methods make qualitative data records slowly and/or process them singly. As you type up your field notes, for example, they are coded and your new understanding reviewed. This new understanding directs your next excursion into the field. It would make no sense to type a year's field notes in your word processor, and only then batch them into NVivo and start coding, linking and writing memos.

If you are able to control the acquisition of data documents, our strong advice is to do so. Qualitative methods are always enhanced by the researcher's ability to learn from the data, before moving on to test emerging ideas in the next record, with further records created by "theoretical sampling", data-driven.

Some researchers, however, do not have the luxury of making, reflecting on and learning from each document before making more data. If you are a historian, or handling documentary analysis, or doing secondary analysis of past interviews, or discourse analysis of existing texts, the data are ready-to-go. The best advice is to batch them in and do basic coding as soon as possible—broad-brush coding, coding by text search and section coding offer alternative ways of initially grappling with larger volumes of text so that you can rapidly access the documents and assess this wealth of data. Then shape the data and plan your exploration of it thoughtfully, sampling within the available pool of data, coding on and/or working set by set.

Import multiple documents

D.I.Y.

To import several documents at once, it is advisable to have them set up so that each can acquire their document name and description from the same place.

- From the Project Pad, choose to Make a Project Document, then to Locate and import readable external text file(s). A Select file to read dialogue will open.

- Locate the folder where your files are stored. (If you are importing files in text only format, remember to change the Files of type option.) Use shift-click or control-click to select the documents you wish to import, then click on Open.

- In the Obtaining document name and description dialogue, choose the option which is appropriate for all of your selected documents.

You will now find your new documents listed in the Document Explorer.

Handling data from multiple sources

While multiple documents imported together are typically of one type, projects often also involve multiple sources of data. Multiple sources can bring many benefits, but they do need to be carefully managed in order to realize those benefits. The goal is to be able to gather all data of a particular type together and to distinguish those from data of other types. You can then ask, for example, how were attitudes to this topic expressed in one-to-one interviews, and whether they were expressed differently in focus groups.

In NVivo there are two primary ways to manage multiple sources of data: using document sets and using document attributes. These are tools which you have begun already to use. In this Part the focus will be on extending their uses as tools for managing and searching data, as well as for working interactively between them. For example, if an attribute for data source is introduced (most efficiently, via a table of attributes, as will be shown below), this can then be used to filter documents to create sets of documents rapidly for the different data sources. Similarly, an imported attribute for cases, used as a filter in the set editor, can code all of a set of documents via the search tool at a case node. This is much less complicated than it sounds, and is a much faster way of placing documents in case nodes than coding them there one by one! The steps will be outlined below, after a few preliminaries. But first we turn attention back to the process of coding, linking and memoing documents, and provide some suggestions for working more efficiently there.

Faster coding

You will find, as you explore the text of further documents, that the rate of creating document memos slows—depending, of course, on how intensively you worked with your first few documents. Gradually your coding also will become more refined. Nodes will be merged, others will be moved, some perhaps to be grouped under an intermediate concept, others may be deleted as no longer being useful. Free Nodes will continue to be sorted and moved into trees.

If the data are fairly homogeneous, then by the time you have coded around six documents, you are likely to find the rate of expansion of your nodes is lessening. You are also very unlikely to be creating whole new trees, unless they come from a reconceptualization of the nodes already created. This means that coding itself (to your probable relief!) will become faster. There are at least two dangers lurking here though:

(a)   The danger that you will not bother to create any more new nodes, but will try to squeeze concepts into existing nodes. How to arrive at a balance between this serious problem—like trying to fit the Ugly Sisters' feet into the fine shoe—and the equally threatening problem of a total proliferation of tiny nodes? If the "squeezing" is a real effort, then don't do it. Remember, NVivo doesn't mind how many nodes you make, and will always merge them later if you discover the shoe did fit. Keep adding to the node memos as you go along as well, especially where you are unsure of the integrity of the coding there.

(b)   The danger that coding will become a task to be completed, a routine that is performed without creative thinking. Lyn calls this "data disposal"—coding in order to get complex data out of your way. When coding becomes data disposal, it is time to stop and consider if anything new is being learned from the additional documents. Or is the problem that you are not giving yourself time to allow your thinking to be stimulated by them? Qualitative coding should almost always be a creative, analytical process, and coding should be regularly "interrupted" by memo writing.

While coding should never be routine, and you will continue to think analytically about your data, growing familiarity with your nodes and their organization assists in making more rapid decisions about which nodes to use in coding particular text. NVivo complements this process with an alternative very rapid method of assigning codes to text: once your nodes are organized in trees, you can code by typing their numeric addresses, rather than by selecting or typing their titles.

Coding by node address

 D.I.Y.

Unless you have a remarkable memory, or a very small number of nodes, work with a list of nodes beside you showing all Tree Nodes with their node addresses and titles (obtained by requesting List all Nodes under the Nodes menu).

- Working in either the Document or Node Browser, highlight the text you wish to code at a Tree Node.

- Type the Tree Node address using the numbers only, with a space between each level. The address will appear in the Speed Coding slot. (No need to put your cursor there.)

- Press Enter on your keyboard to complete the coding process. The full title of your node will be shown in the Speed Coding slot, giving you an opportunity to quickly check it was the right node!

Tip · If you are routinely coding at both Tree Nodes and Free Nodes, have your Coder showing the Free Nodes so that they are easily accessible for coding, while at the same time using the node addresses for coding at Tree Nodes.

There are several short documents you might sample from at this stage as you try coding using Tree Node addresses. Andrew was a research student in biology. He is talking about the ebb and flow of his interest in research as he moves from university to industry and back again. Professors D and S, at the other end of the academic spectrum, each reflect back to a quite different critical factor that influenced their development as researchers. Barbara heads up a successful commercial business offering analytical research services, offering a contrast to the academic researchers.

In the **Researchers 5** project, choose first of all to Make a Project Document, importing (at the same time) the documents Andrew, Barbara, Professor D and Professor S, located in the Source Documents folder for this version of the project. Before coding you will, of course, need to print out a list of the nodes so that you can easily see what their addresses are. Then, as you code using the Tree Node addresses, you will find that you are able to work much more quickly than before and as your familiarity with the addresses increases you will really pick up speed in applying the codes.

Coding with Text Search

Like any other search in NVivo, text search finds words or phrases in the text, and codes the resulting finds at a node.

You can specify what context the coding is spread to. The means it is a way of getting coding done fast!

You may simply wish to code at a node every time a person is mentioned, a topic is raised or a question asked. You may come upon a new concept or category for which you wish to make a node, and then wonder whether it really is the first time it has come up or whether it was there before, but you just didn't see it. Text search can be used to check whether, indeed, such things were mentioned elsewhere—providing there are keywords that can be used to "get a handle" on those concepts or categories. And it will do more than just find them.

Text search nodes, like any other node, can be browsed for recoding and coding-on. Having been pointed to potentially relevant sections of your documents, you can check the context of those sections, determine just exactly what is relevant, and code accordingly. What text search is doing, then, is alerting you to where in your data you might access material about the concept or category of interest, so that you can then capture it in a node and continue analysis from there. Note that text search, like any search, can be pointed to exactly the documents or parts of documents you want to search. And if you are using it to check where you might have missed coding, it can be incorporated into a Boolean Difference search so that all those passages you had already noted and coded are excluded from the results.

Thus text search can be used to locate and/or verify whether an expression has or has not been used, or perhaps to compare usage of, say, different pronouns or expressions in particular contexts, that is, to test ideas from and in the data rather than simply to code.

NVivo can be asked to search more widely, for any of several alternative words or phrases at the same time. This way of searching is often more useful to qualitative studies, where it is likely that there will be more than one word that will point to the text you are interested in. Finds for any of the words listed will be included together in a text search results node. But watch for the distinctiveness of the words you ask NVivo to search for! A search for media could also turn up immediately, for example.

Searching for an exact word or phrase

- From the Project Pad, choose Search Project Database. NVivo's Search Tool will open.

- Click on the icon next to Text Search. A Text Search dialogue will open over the top part of the Search Tool.

- Type, into the slot at the top of the dialogue, the word or phrase you wish to search for in your text. Leave other options as they are for this search. Click OK at the bottom of the Text Search dialogue.

- Specify the Scope for your search: do you want to search All Documents, or just a particular set of documents (or nodes)?

- Click Run Search at the bottom of the Search Tool.

When the search is complete, choose to Browse Node. Oops! All you have in the node is the exact string that was searched for. You can, of course, gain access to the text around each find (using the right mouse button menu), but it might be more useful to see a little more right from the start. At least that will allow you to determine whether finds are totally unwanted.

To view context

- In the Node Browser, use Ctrl A (Select All) to highlight all the finds at that node.

- From your context menu, choose View Enclosing Paragraph.

NVivo will display the enclosing paragraphs for every find, showing the additional text in a different color. This allows you to see more easily where the word or phrase you were searching for is located in the text, without the additional text having been automatically coded there.

Review each of the finds and determine whether you wish to keep them or not. Code additional text to the node for each find you keep (the search results node is already listed in the Speed Coding slot.)

Alternatively:

Re-run the search, but this time, before clicking on Run Search:

- Click on Customise Result near the base of the Search Tool.

- Choose to Spread finds in a scope document to: Enclosing paragraph. Note another option you might choose is to type in a Number of Characters you want (e.g. 50).

- Click OK. On the Search Tool, Use Custom Handling will now be checked.

- Click on Run Search. Your results will be placed in a new node, as a child of Search Results in the Trees area. Note you could collect the finds into any other node you choose - automatically merging the coding with that node.

Tip
In the Node Explorer, note that the new node has been given a description based on how it was created. If the results of the search were useful, rename the node, and perhaps move it elsewhere in your trees.

Searching for multiple words or phrases

- In the Search Tool, click on Text Search.

- Check the Use Wildcards option in the Text Search dialogue. Type the first word or phrase you wish to search for in your text. Click on the > symbol next to Add special character. Choose the alteration character …|…, the last listed.

  Or, type in the | character using your keyboard—it is usually located above the backslash (on the key above Enter).

- Add your alternative word or phrase. You can add further alternation characters and words, if you wish.

- Continue to set up your search by choosing the options you want, as before.

- Browse your results, and use the ability to see context and code further text to maximize the benefit of your text search.

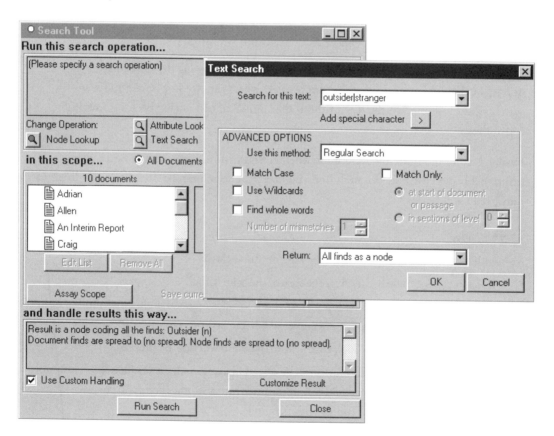

Combining text and other searches

In all of the Boolean and Proximity search operators, you can ask for combinations of searches for text, coding and attributes. This allows much more subtle searching of text, retrieving for example only the words that occur in particular discussions, or in documents from interviews in one social area. Use a Boolean search to find occurrences of a word that have not yet been coded at the node for that category.

Excluding what has been coded already

D.I.Y.

- In the Search Tool, choose to run a Boolean Search, with Difference (Less) as the Operator.

- Under Find text referenced by any of these items... select Choose Text Patterns....

- In the following dialogue, type in your search expression, with whatever options you wish to use. Click on Add Pattern, so that it shows in the pane to the right of the dialogue (remember to click Use Wildcards if you wish to specify multiple phrases using the alternation character).

- Click OK to return to the Boolean Search dialogue, where you will see the text pattern now showing in the top pane.

- Under ...but by none of these items, select Choose Nodes. Add the node or nodes which already hold coding for the concept you are searching for. Click OK to return them to the Boolean Search dialogue, then OK again to return to the Search Tool.

- Set the scope for your search (you may wish to leave this at All Documents in this case).

- Use Custom Handling to spread the finds to, say, 50 characters either side. This will give you enough to assess whether the find is worth pursuing, without overwhelming you with long passages of text.

- Inspect the results, and code-on as necessary.

Research is often sheer hard work, involving repetitive or uninspiring tasks (try cutting several hundred tissue samples for slides, or filling a thousand envelopes!), yet it is also something to be enjoyed…but in what way is it enjoyed, and by whom? Use text search to delve into the phenomenology of this experience by searching, initially, for the word "enjoy", using the data you now have in the **Researchers** 5 database. Then (into a new node) try re-running the search with what had already been coded at the node <u>enjoyment</u> excluded from the search and compare the results with your first search.

To "tidy" the results from the second search (which will be listed as a Difference search in your Search Results Tree), go through the finds discarding those that are irrelevant (such as the words of Denise's question to the research students). Code any finds that usefully add to your understanding of how researchers might enjoy research directly to the existing node for enjoyment. Note that once you have coded the first useful find to that node, it will continue to show in the Speed Coding slot, so coding will require only that you select the text you want (which may require seeking additional context using the right mouse menu), then click on Code or press Enter.

Autocoding by section

The quickest coding is achieved with the Section Coder, which will "autocode" sections of the text under nodes made for each of the headings used in the text, thus in one swoop creating the nodes, determining the context (i.e. sections) and doing the coding. You can set it to create the nodes either by the order and level of the sections that are in the documents, or by the titles of the sections (e.g. name of speaker). Each of these forms of section coding achieves a quite different result, so they are appropriate for different tasks or data.

Coding by section number requires that all documents to be coded that way are set up with exactly the same structure of headings and sections. It is therefore ideal for survey data, and benefits from the use of a document template to guarantee uniformity in preparation of the documents. Assuming the content of the questions are being placed in Tree 1, and Heading 1 style was used for main questions with Heading 2 for subquestions, it will result in the answers from all respondents to Question 1 being placed at Node (1 1), those to Question 2 going in to Node (1 2), the answers to Question 2 (b) into Node (1 2 2), and so on.

Coding by section title does not require any uniformity across documents, but expects that there will be repeated use of the same headings, as occurs, for example, when there are multiple speakers in a focus group, or a series of interviews that cover the same topics but not necessarily in the same order. Thus, assuming that speaker identifiers have been used as headings in the focus group transcript (and with no subsections under them), all that was said by each person will be gathered into a single node with their speaker identifier as its title. (If multiple focus groups are conducted, make sure you use unique speaker identifiers for members of each group!)

In either case, where subsections exist, the heading only (or the heading and just that text appearing before the first subheading) will be coded. If there is a need to code all the text at that level as well, this can easily be achieved. Thus, in a focus group, if you have used headings for both the topic being discussed and (at a lower level of heading style) who is speaking, you will be able to gather the text separately for both topic and speaker.

Preparation

D.I.Y.

- For each of the two examples below, you need to create a new Tree Node (using either the Create Nodes dialogue, or in the Node Explorer using the context menu) below which you can place the nodes that will be generated by the Section Coder. (Note the address of that node!)

- Check the documents' formatting; will the sections properly identify material you wish to code?

- Import (as a batch, if they are surveys) the new documents you wish to code by section.

Coding by section number

- From the list of All Documents in the Document Explorer, select (highlight) one of your survey documents, then in the Document menu, click on Code by Section....

- In the Section Coder dialogue, type the address for the Tree Node you have just created into the Parent tree-node slot (or click on Choose and select it from the list of nodes). Click OK.

- Repeat these two steps for as many surveys as you have imported (note: a multiple select option is being planned for this function).

- Go to your Node Explorer, and expand Trees so that you can see the new Sections (Questions) node. It will now have a + next to it, indicating it has children. Expand it and you will find that it has a child node for every new heading found in your document. They will be arranged in parallel structure to the outline of the sections in your document.

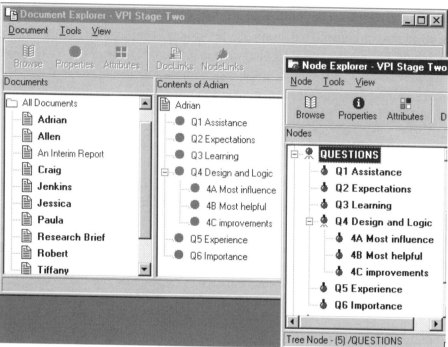

Now you are able to see at a glance what every respondent answered to Q1 (and each other question). You might then simply "split" these by values on an attribute (see below), or code-on as you focus on the topic of that question. Later, you might ask whether something that was said arose in response to that question, or to another.

Coding by section title

- From the list of All Documents in the Document Explorer, select a focus group (or similar) document, then in the Document menu, click on Code by Section....

- In the Section Coder dialogue, change the selection to Code sections by title. Type the address for the Tree Node you have just created into the Parent tree-node slot (or click on Choose and select it from the list of nodes). Click OK.

- Go to your Node Explorer, and expand Trees so that you can see your new node. It will now have a + next to it, indicating it has children. Expand it and you will find that it has a child node for every different heading found in your document. These will include both topics and speakers, if you had both.

- Browse any of the speaker nodes, and you will find there all that person said during the course of the focus group, (so long as the subheadings were the same for each of the speeches).

- Browse a topic node, and you will probably find just the series of headings. Use Ctrl-A to select all the headings at once. From your context menu, choose View Enclosing Section. All of the subsections for that topic for the whole document will come into view, in differently colored text.

- Select all the text again (Ctrl-A), and click Code, to code all the additional text to the node for that topic (this node will automatically be showing in the Speed Coding slot).

If you have more than one focus group covering the same topics, then defer expanding the topic sections until all group documents have been section coded.

Now, by browsing the section nodes, you are able to review everything said in each of your groups about the topics covered. And having coded all that each speaker said, you can now review those nodes and note whether it was the same person who repeatedly used a particular expression, or note the way in which particular group members contributed to the group process, or were influenced by it.

One of the focus groups run for this project has been treated as a proxy document, but transcripts for two others have been imported into **Researchers 5** (PhD students and Focus 3). Use these two to practise coding by section title, and to explore the benefits of having all that is said by a person gathered at a node for that person.

Faster attributes

Earlier, we noted the crucial difference between the conceptual act of coding (creating a topic category and recording there the data that belongs) and the descriptive task of storing information. Attributes were created for documents in Part 3.

You now have quite a collection of documents in your project, and doubtless a lot of coding to do. Putting in the information you have about each document may be a simple matter of a few clicks as you first import or browse each one, or it may be more tedious because of the amount of information you have available about that document. If your study also involved a quantitative data collection, you may want to import salient variables from your statistical database, to use as attribute data in your qualitative analysis. Consider then, setting up your document attribute data in a table and importing it all in one step, rather than having to add the information document by document. (Note that attribute data can be imported in a parallel way for nodes as well—to be discussed in the context of using Cases, below.)

There are two steps to this process. In the first, you need to prepare your data in table-based software, such as Excel. The Appendix provides details of how to do this. In the second step, you will import the data into NVivo. If the table you are importing includes attributes with different types of values (say, most are strings but some are numeric), this will require an additional preparatory step.

Preparing for importing attributes

- Prepare your data in Excel (or other table-based software) as per instructions in the Appendix. Save your file in text only format.

- *If your attributes are mostly of one value type, with just one or two of a different type:* Create those attributes which are different from the majority interactively (i.e. using the menus) in NVivo, *before* importing the table (no need to specify values, just the attribute name and value type). Make sure their names are typed in exactly the same way (including capitalization) as they will appear in your table.

- *If you have a larger number of attributes for each type* (e.g. several string attributes, and also several numeric attributes): Set these up in two separate tables, e.g. one for the strings, and another for the numerics, so they can be imported separately.

Import your attribute table into NVivo

- From the Documents menu at the very top of your screen, choose Import Document Attributes...

- At the top of the Document attribute import dialogue, where it says File to import, click on Choose.

- Navigate through your directories to find and select the text file version of the table you have created.

- Check through the options offered for handling attributes in the Document attribute import dialogue.

- If a document title is not recognized: You can choose to allow NVivo to create any documents that do not yet exist (the default option). For those who plan to prepare their documents in NVivo, this provides a rapid method of creating multiple documents. Those who plan to import further documents should select the option Ignore the data for that document to avoid the situation where they set up parallel documents within the program (one renamed and with text, the other with attribute data). If further documents are imported there is no problem in re-importing an attribute table in order to update the new documents with attributes.

- If an attribute name is not recognised: If you are importing other than String attributes, you will need to change the selection for Attribute type.

- Click OK. You will be given a message: Attribute import successful.

- View your imported data by choosing Explore all Document Attributes from the Project Pad. If you had your Attribute Explorer open during the import process, you will need to close and reopen it to see the added attribute data.

- You are now able to view and manipulate your attribute data in tabular format within NVivo through the Attribute Explorer (as described in Part 3).

You will find a table of document attributes for all the interviews in the Researchers project located in the Source Documents folder for **Researchers 5** (C:\QSR Projects\Researchers 5\All Users\Source Documents\resdocdata.txt). First create a number attribute for *age* using the menus, then import the attribute table. You will find that you now have many more demographic attributes stored for your documents, as well as an attribute for data source. The latter will allow comparisons of what is said, for example, about intellectual stimulation, across different types of data.

Faster Sets

We have made sets of documents and nodes so far in the simplest possible way, dragging and dropping in the Explorers. But NVivo has a finer tool for making, changing and filtering items in sets, a tool that has a "hotlink" to the scope of a search. Indeed, you have already met the Document and Node Set Editors, as you have chosen to limit searches to particular (already created) sets of documents or nodes. But now that you have a larger number and range of documents, you will find the Document Set Editor more efficient also for making new sets. As an alternative to dragging documents to a set in the Document Explorer, you can use the values of an attribute (or some other criterion) to filter your documents, saving the result as a new set. This is particularly useful where there are a number of documents to be selected, or where you are not sure which documents meet the criteria you want to establish for belonging to the set.

Use set filtering to make a new set

- On the Project Pad, ensure the Documents tab is active. On the right side, click on the Sets tab, and then on Make or Change a Document Set to open the Document Set Editor.

- In the Documents in: slot above the right pane, select Working Set. If the Set contains any documents, then choose Select All, then Remove, to clear the set.

- In the left pane, select the set of All Documents. This pane should now be active.

- Click on Filter Documents. Choose whether you want documents coded by a particular node (they will be selected if coded anywhere with that node), or perhaps documents with a particular attribute, such as their <u>data source</u>.

- Click Select at the base of the Set Editor. The documents which meet this criterion will be selected. Click Copy>> to move them to the right pane.

- Click in the right pane to make it active, then on Save As at the top of the dialogue. Type in a name for the set, and click OK. Close the Document Set Editor.

  A parallel process can be used to create Node Sets—perhaps to locate the set of nodes that code your literature, or a particular document.

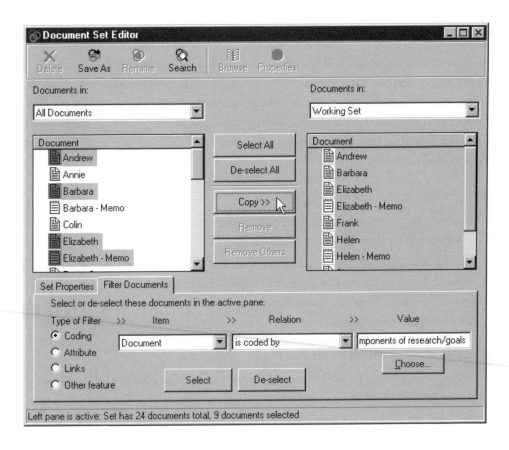

Now that you have many more documents in **Researchers 5**, and you have imported attributes for them—one of which was an attribute for data source—use that attribute to add new documents to the Set already created for Interviews (watch how you manage that in the Set Editor!) and to create a new Set for Focus Groups.

Faster cases

If you have started to use case nodes, as they were introduced earlier (Part 5), you are probably coding text into them interactively, one segment or document at a time. Now that you have learned to use the section coder, and to use attributes to filter sets, there are faster ways you can create and move text into case nodes. Indeed, the fastest way to create case nodes in the first place may be to begin by importing a table of node attributes for named cases (see below).

D.I.Y.

Coding text (partial documents) at case nodes

- Revisit coding by section title (above) to work out a strategy to autocode the text of focus groups or other relevant documents.

- Drag nodes created with the Section Coder (e.g. for participants) from their Tree to a Case Type node (where they will become a Case under that Case Type), or use Cut and Paste to move them there. If the case nodes already exist, then use Cut and Merge Node to add the additional text to the case node.

Coding sets of documents at a case node

- When you are creating your document attribute table, add an attribute for <u>cases</u>, with values that define which case node each document is to go into. For example, if you have carried out multiple interviews with Jennifer over time (or with multiple people about Jennifer), then under the cases attribute, give each of these the value Jennifer.

- Use a value for the cases attribute (e.g. Jennifer) as a filter to create a set of documents for that case. Send the set to the search tool (no need to save it first). They will appear as the scope documents in the search tool.

- Under the scope panels, choose the option to Save current scope as: Node. A Choose Node dialogue will open.

- Using the drop-down list and panel in the Choose Nodes dialogue, choose the appropriate Case Node (e.g. Jennifer) for the set of documents showing in the scope. Click OK, and your documents are now coded at the selected case node.

- Repeat for each value of the cases attribute, until all documents are coded at their respective case nodes.

It is best to have the destination nodes already created (you might use a node attribute table to do so—see below) before trying to place the documents, especially if you are doing this for a number of cases. But if you forget to do so, you can create a new case node (but not name it) by clicking on the star (create) icon ✳ in the Choose Node dialogue.

Importing Attributes for Case Nodes

Nodes too can have attributes. To give attributes to a Case Node (e.g. for each participant in a focus group, or each pupil in a school) allows demographic and other variable information to be applied to parts of documents, whereas document attributes apply to whole documents. Then you could ask for example about the contribution made on a topic by participants in different age groups.

As with document attributes, node attributes and their values can be created interactively (the process is exactly symmetrical with the document attribute creation). If you create a node attribute with the same name as a document attribute, NVivo will recognise it and you will be asked if you want to use the same values. But also, as with document attributes, you can create and import node attributes from a table prepared in a spreadsheet or similar program.

Once values of an attribute have been given to a node (such as a Case Node), any text coded to that node (at any time) will acquire those attributes. Additionally, attribute values assigned to a Case Type Node will be acquired by any *new* Cases created thereafter under that Case Type (of value where there are a number of Case Type nodes each with cases under them). With a little advance planning, the Case Type Nodes and Case Nodes can be created and assigned attributes all in one go, by creating and importing a carefully constructed Node Attribute table. They are then ready to have documents (or part documents) coded at them, as outlined above.

Importing attributes for existing case nodes

- Follow the basic instructions for preparing a Node Attribute table, given in the Appendix.

- Note that the format for a case node title uses a full stop in front of the case type, and a colon in front of the case, thus .Schools.Penrose:Julie

- Save your table in the usual way (i.e. first in its native format, then as text only).

- In NVivo, from the Nodes menu at the top of your screen, choose Import Node Attributes...

- At the top of the Node attribute import dialogue, where it says File to import, click on Choose. Navigate through your directories to find and select the text file version of the table you have created.

- Change the first of the default options in the Node attribute import dialogue, so that If a node title is not recognized NVivo will Ignore data for that node.

- Click OK. You will be given a message: Attribute import successful.

- View your imported data by choosing Explore all Node Attributes from the Project Pad. Note that if you had your Attribute Explorer open during the import process, you will need to close and reopen it to see the attribute data.

Using a table to create Case Nodes and assign Case Type values

- In the first column (headed Node) list the names firstly for each of the Case Type nodes. To format a Case Type node, type a full stop immediately in front of its title, so that Penrose, as a Case Type under Schools, would appear as .Schools.Penrose

- After you have listed the Case Type nodes, add the Case Nodes to each line in the first column. Specific titles for the Case Nodes are preceded by a colon, so that Julie at Penrose School will appear as .Schools.Penrose:Julie

- Enter the attribute names, and the specific values for each case type and each case, as for any attribute table.

- Save your table in the usual way (i.e. first in its native format, then as tab separated text).

- In the Project Pad, from the Nodes menu, choose Import Node Attributes...

- At the top of the Node attribute import dialogue, where it says File to import, click on Choose. Navigate through your directories to find and select the text version of the table.

- Retain the default options in the Node attribute import dialogue. The first of these means that the nodes will be created if they do not exist.

Check the Cases area in your Node Explorer, to see all the new case nodes. Check in the Attribute Explorer that attribute values have been assigned as you expected. Now as you code documents to your new Case Nodes, as outlined above, the appropriate values of attributes will be applied.

 If you create a case type node, e.g. "Penrose"—and give it values of an attribute, e.g. social status, all cases you create under it will inherit that value.

Faster searches

Well no, not really! But having attributes, sets and where appropriate, cases does make it possible to ask fresh questions of the data, sometimes in an exploratory mode, sometimes more interpretively. So their value extends beyond simply being tools for managing data, to being tools to assist in interrogating the data.

Each provides for a different kind of use when it comes to asking questions of the data: *Sets* are used for scoping searches and reports and are therefore ideal for asking questions about a subset of the data; *Attributes* can be included as items in searches, and are therefore ideal for asking comparative questions about the data; *Cases* bring together multiple documents or part documents and data from multiple sources, so that by undertaking within-case or cross-case analyses you can ask questions about processes within a "bounded" entity, and compare that entity with others of the same type.

Using attributes to make comparisons

Attribute values invite comparisons, for example: "Was there a gendered response to this question?" "What do my different sources of data say about this issue?" "Does a person's level of [scaled variable] make a difference to their experience of that situation?" Group membership (defined by attribute values) in these situations is categorical information, but what members of each group might have said on an issue is qualitative information. NVivo can take the qualitative text on a particular subject, and "split" it into new nodes based on the categories of the grouping variable, thus allowing comparison of the text across groups.

Because attribute data applies to whole documents, the text at any node in a document must intersect with the attribute value(s) that apply to that document. Searches involving attributes therefore typically use the Boolean Matrix Intersection operator. You can elect to take one node and intersect it with the values of an attribute, making a table of results with multiple cells across a single row, or you could examine a whole set of nodes (e.g. all the subcategories, or children, in one tree) in relation to all the values of an attribute, making for a full cross tabulation with many rows and columns. While the latter is useful to provide an overview of patterns (e.g. by examining the number of documents coded in each cell), it can be more confusing when you wish to examine the text in the cells—simply because of the number of cells and amount of data available. In such situations, you are often better off to take one issue, or one situation, and examine that in relation to the values of the attribute of interest before moving on to look in detail at another.

A matrix with attributes

- From the Project Pad, choose to Search Project Database.

Run this search operation...

- In the Search Tool, click on the search icon next to Boolean Search.

- For your Operator: choose Matrix Intersection. The dialogue will expand to provide options for two sets of search items.

- Under Find text referenced by these items... click on Choose Nodes. In the Choose Nodes dialogue, find, highlight and add the nodes you want to examine across groups.

- Under ...pairwise with each of these items, click on Choose Attribute Values.

- In the Choose Attribute Values dialogue, double-click on Document Attributes, then on the attribute you are interested in using to split your data. The values it can take will be expanded below it. Select the values you wish to examine and move them to the right pane.

A node's children or subtree can be added. A range of an attribute's values can be added using "greater than or less than" (for text as well as numbers).

- Click OK to return to the Search Tool.

in this scope...

- Set the scope for your search to the document set you wish to search (probably, All non-memo documents. Run Search!

The search results are stored in children of the node: (x x) /Search results/Matrix Intersection.

- Click OK. You will be taken to a display of the results of the search, set out in table format to show the cross-tabulation of items selected. Items from the first pool (the node/s) define the rows of the cross-tabulation, and items from the second pool (values of an attribute) define the columns.

- From the pull-down list in the slot next to Display, select Number of documents coded (or an alternative option). Numbers will appear in the cells in your table, and they will become shaded to indicate the density of coding.

- Click on a cell of the table and choose Browse/Code Node to open the Node Browser for that cell. Compare what is there with the text at another cell in the same row.

Examining the interaction of attributes

Often attributes are interrelated. It may be difficult to tell, for example, whether apparent differences in an academic's experience of research is more to do with their gender or their discipline, or whether it is the combination of these interrelated variables that matters, rather than one *or* the other. Use of a Matrix Intersection search scoped to the node of interest can provide an answer to this much more complex question.

A matrix of attributes

D.I.Y.

- Choose to intersect the values of one attribute with the values of another (Boolean Search: Matrix Intersection).

- Choose Custom Scope then Remove All documents and Edit List for Nodes.

- In the Node Set Editor, select the node of interest, Copy>> to the empty Working Set. Click on the Search icon to return to the Search Tool.

- Run the search.

Consider the text in each cell of the resulting matrix to determine whether reports of experience (or whatever the text coded at the scope node was about) vary for different combinations of the values of these attributes. Note that it is possible (though less likely) that an interactive effect could be revealed even where there is no apparent effect from either attribute on its own.

Use the **Researchers 5** project, with the document attribute data imported, or **Researchers 6**, to examine firstly, whether gender is associated with some aspect of the experience of being a researcher, for example, one's experience of passion for research, or intellectual challenge. Then consider the impact of discipline alone, before looking at the interaction of gender and discipline, with respect to that aspect of the researchers' experience. If you examine the interaction of these attributes, you will then be able to tell, for example, whether being a female in science is different from being a male in science with respect to, say, one's experience of passion for research, or intellectual challenge, or one's rationale for being involved in research at all; and whether this is paralleled by the experience of social scientists, or whether being female rather than male in social science has different implications.

You might also find it interesting to examine whether there is a gendered view on what research is about. Beware, though, just interpreting on the basis of number of documents. Elizabeth is coded at *discovery* but browsing the text reveals that this was not her own viewpoint.

Taking Stock

A much bigger project, very fast! But if the tools have been well used, it is a less unruly project than earlier versions when there was virtually no data!

Critical processes in qualitative research defy speed; they require reflection and review. While some data processing tasks are not intrinsically qualitative, having them done may enhance enquiry processes and, if the shaping tools are familiar, it is worth exploring which processes can be speeded up. Coding by text search gives you automatic categorizing that is no replacement for reading and thinking about your data (none of NVivo's tools offer that!) but certainly a swift means of getting access to the data and providing for coding-on later, when meanings are clearer, and you have a gap in the pressure and excitement of data buildup. Batching of document import, section coding and table import of attributes automate clerical processes so you can get on with the interpretive ones.

This Part has shown how rapidly these processes can give access to your data, in ways that can be immediately productive and immediately show it to you anew, so you can review, and re-view all or some data, revisit and revise the theories that you are tentatively sketching. Now, back to interpretation.

Part 9: Getting there

Where is "there" and how will you know when you arrive? The answer depends on where you started. Projects differ in design and purpose, and qualitative methods differ widely in their account of what is an acceptable outcome of research. But the processes of getting to the appropriate "there" have a lot in common, and all can use tools for conceptual development, for surprise and discovery and for pattern seeking and validating. In this Part, we discuss ways of reviewing your goals, then of using those tools for your purposes. We conclude with a section on reporting what you discovered, when you do get there.

Aiming for and achieving research goals

It is not unusual for qualitative projects to start without an explicit research question, or to end by asking a question that was not considered at the beginning. So you may have commenced this book with a project but no picture of the theory or explanation that would complete it. At the extremes, the aims of analysis may be very pragmatic (knowing what is going on here) or very abstract (construction of a new theory of this phenomenon). But these aims, and all the range between, have in common that the researcher is seeking an analytical outcome *from* the data.

Qualitative methods do however share processes of arrival, and there are tools in NVivo for each of these. For many researchers the goal is "saturation" of concepts, the sense that nothing new is coming up. For this purpose they need techniques of continuous massaging of the categories and thinking about them. For almost all, at some stage, the goal is an arrival at surprise and discovery—something new and unexpected. They will do so through revisiting data in new approaches, writing and reviewing memos. Most researchers seek and attempt to find and validate patterns, discover and account for relationships and test explanations, locate cases that don't fit, interrogate trends. They will do so through increasingly flexible use of the search processes, teasing data out, interrogating associations, focusing on finer contexts.

Just as in Part 6 we could not teach how to "emerge" a theory, so too in this Part we are unable to offer a recipe for the theory that will make sense of any particular data. The nearer you get to the conclusion of your own project, the less likely it is that any general book can tell you what to do to arrive. So what we offer at this stage are things you can try, in your search for ways of arrival.

Categories and theory

All qualitative research needs tools for "emerging" the categories with which analysis can be conducted and theories constructed (Part 6). But the goal of "theory" is the Lorelei of qualitative research students. In recent parts, we have dealt with tools for managing and ordering concepts and drawing together the vocabulary of categories whose relationships to the data are explored and tested (Part 7). The project built momentum as processes were speeded up (as described in Part 8), and for most researchers this gives a sense that they are getting somewhere. But how will you know when you are there, and especially, when you have a theory?

At the start of this book we warned that it cannot teach any particular method. This means of course that we can't tell how to get to the appropriate "there" for your methodological approach. At this stage, we urge you again to return to your methodological literature, and particularly to examples of how projects achieve their goals. You may find, now that you are deep in your own data, that completed projects offer startling parallels, or surprise you with relevant concepts.

Whilst you may well have started without knowing what you were seeking, now you need to know. Return to the Project Journal and add memos on what a satisfactory outcome would be like. What are you aiming for? What would that elusive "theory" be like if you met it? If these questions puzzle, ask instead "What do I want to be able to *say*, and why would anyone believe me?"

We start with tools for reviewing where you are going.

The project and its purposes

At this stage, it is often beneficial to revisit the research goals and ensure that the analysis process is aiming accurately for them. We have warned earlier of the perils of ritualistic research, coding that is treated as an end in itself, or editing that is cosmetic rather than analytic. At this stage in a project, the effects of data processing without purpose will become evident and now is the time to deal with them!

Thoughtfully review the project, in terms of purpose. Since qualitative research almost always seeks an outcome that isn't known when you start, some superfluity is built into the method. All of us find at this stage that we have been coding at categories that don't matter or are duplicated and at least some of the attributes stored aren't relevant for asking the questions that now dominate the project. As you become more assured, you can confidently focus data processing and as it is focused it will become more analytical. (Revisit the discussion of coding in Part 4, and become very critical of coding that seems boring or ritualistic; coding at this stage should be perpetually relevant and interesting!)

 Conduct a review of purpose and processing

D.I.Y.

In Part 2 we commenced with a Project Journal. If this has been maintained as a research record, you might now revisit it and record your review of your purposes and the progress of your data processing.

- Browse the Project Journal and date and edit a new section on *Research purposes and data processing*. Record your interpretation of your achievements so far and where you think your project is now going. Note critical concepts and ideas derived from the data, and finally, identify those things that still need attention. Use all the abilities of compound documents to draw together each aspect of the project.

- Use DataBites to external files to link into your review any triumphal interim reports or worried memos you've been writing about your progress.

- Review the questions you have been asking throughout the project. Use DocLinks to memos where questions are recorded, noting those worthy of further consideration given where the project is now going. (Mark critical documents and memos with coloured icons.)

- Use NodeLinks to provide rapid access to critical nodes, or to those identified as needing further evaluation.

- Check those documents for which the coding is inadequate or requires review in the light of your evaluation. Use DocLinks or Node Extracts to point to documents or quotes which are pertinent to your growing sense of direction.

- Record memos on any themes or questions that you now recall as pertinent but which your data processing so far seems to have evaded. (Yes there will be some!)

You are likely to find your project is now much more firmly directed. Now you can start asking the questions that will lead to the desired outcome.

Are your concepts good enough?

Good enough for what? Your methods literature will answer that. But only you can evaluate them. You are likely to have decided at this stage that the concepts require sharpening and focusing.

The first critical issue may be whether you have developed and explored the core concepts thoroughly. What may work now is a return to the data available for each of the categories, rethinking, rereading and re-viewing the coded text. This would lead to development and rewriting and now coding of memos. Aim for the maturing of your central concepts, going beyond your initial coding to purposive category development.

The second aspect of concept review is to look at the framework of concepts as a whole, and tighten it. This activity serves as a "clean up" of nodes. It has two purposes: it serves to clarify the concepts that have been identified in the project, and it prepares your coding to support more complex searching of patterns.

Concept clarification

You are likely to find you are now working in a different relationship with some of your concepts. Whatever your method, the processes of making sense of the data involve concept development and selection: in NVivo terms, this means some nodes are becoming more central than others. For these, it becomes particularly important to clarify what they represent and whether there are multiple concepts hiding in one node.

D.I.Y.

Clarifying in the Node Browser

Use the Node Browser for synthesis, review and writing about the concepts you have developed:

- Select a central node. Browse it, reread and rethink the material coded there, to ensure that it all "belongs".

- Write a new memo, or add to an existing memo recording the picture you developed of that concept as you read through the text.

- Very critically review the coded material as a whole. View the context of any segment that surprises, or jump to its source document. Why was that text coded here (and why not the surrounding text)? If a segment no longer belongs (or never did!) it can now be recoded and/or deleted from this node.

- Actively seek dimensions of the concept; challenge its simplicity. Are there subtle differences in the coded material? Are there sub-categories to be explored? If the answer is yes, create new nodes, and code-on from the Node Browser to the finer categories or separate concepts.

- Ask about saturation. Is nothing different coming up? Or is the text "active", still changing and shifting. Keep these ideas in memos.

Memo writing (linked to the nodes being reviewed) is particularly important during this clean up process, as reading through nodes prompts many questions about the data and the issues of the project in the alert researcher's mind. Memos (and descriptions) can also serve as a rapid reminder of what a node is about, should you puzzle over it again later.

My initial thinking about intellectual challenge, influenced both by personal experience and reading of the literature, was of people being stimulated by the excitement of tackling and working through new ideas. When I looked at what I had coded at the node for challenge, I found the text was largely to do with the kinds of struggles people found and faced in doing research—much more prosaic things like difficulties in writing, in organizing their thoughts, and so on. This made it necessary to rethink what the node was about and where it might fit in my conceptual system.

Conceptual framework review

In Part 7 we discussed ways of organizing nodes. As your project develops, you may find it worth reviewing the nodes not just as a catalogue of concepts but also as an indication of a conceptual framework.

Re-view the node system as a whole

D.I.Y.

A list of nodes with descriptions is an advantage. As you review how your conceptual framework relates to your purposes, you may wish to return and report the review in your project document.

- List all the nodes, with descriptions and coding reported.

- Save the list of nodes, which NVivo dates for you, as a rich text file.

- Browse the Project Journal and start a section on node review. Place a DataBite linking the section to the external file that is a current list of nodes, and record your reflections on the nodes that now frame your study. What are the sorts of nodes you are making? Do these relate to the sorts of questions your study is designed to answer? (Do this repetitively and you will have a valuable project history growing in the Project Journal.)

- Review the logical elegance of the tree structure (as in Part 7).

Review the performance of nodes

The review so far has been of how the concepts work as a framework for your project. A second stage of review will move you further towards your analytical goals. Having clarified the coding content of nodes, ask now what you are doing with them.

Some, perhaps many nodes may be providing situational context—about the broad issue being discussed or the setting or social context, for example. These will generally code large passages and serve only as a basis for asking about occurrences of finer topics coded at other nodes. (When this issue of curriculum review is discussed by teachers in relation to school organization, do they offer a different view from discussion in the context of pupil needs?) You don't expect much from these nodes, except that they are there, and your coding at them reliable, when you want to ask about the context.

Coding at a node should never be the end of analysis, always a beginning. It offers a first gathering of material, for re-viewing and reflecting. We share a concern at queries like, "How can I get a print-out of the text of all my nodes?" To do so wastes a lot of pine trees, since your research purpose is highly unlikely to be merely a summary of everything about a series of topics. Such a summary is merely descriptive, and qualitative research is almost always seeking analysis. From the print-out you can only describe the quoted material, since it is dead data. You can't recontextualize the segments coded at a node, or return from them to rethink the document, or move forward to develop the category theoretically as you code at finer dimensions, or ask *who* had this attitude, and what *conditions* seem to encourage it. If your use of nodes has been merely to print them out and summarize what's there, try the following exercise.

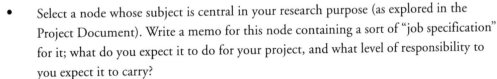

Reflect on particular nodes

D.I.Y.
- Select a node whose subject is central in your research purpose (as explored in the Project Document). Write a memo for this node containing a sort of "job specification" for it; what do you expect it to do for your project, and what level of responsibility to you expect it to carry?
- Make a new model containing this node. Place in the model the other nodes, documents or other items whose relation to your node you have to understand. Try layering the model to represent different ways these relations might be interpreted.

- Now conduct a sort of "performance review" on the node. How has it been functioning? Evaluate the data coded at this node in terms of its ability to do the job. How must it develop if it is to carry its purpose satisfactorily? You may now wish to return to recode some data, in the light of this review, seeking a broader coverage, or looking for the particular themes that now appear crucially important.

- Focus on nodes which have become unimportant, either because they are getting little coding or because they seem no longer related to the emergent issues of the project. Look at these together (do they indicate a forgotten aspect of the project?).

- Review choices for dealing with these nodes. You might leave them there but place them in a set so they can be revisited. You might move them into a tree of "Past nodes". You might merge them with nodes that are more inclusive, or simply delete them if you are confident of their irrelevance. (Treat this as a last resort. Never waste work if it might be useful!)

What of the nodes that code more specific issues or processes? How are they performing in the analysis process? Review your use of the central nodes: are they allowing you to penetrate the complexity of your data and make sense of it?

Concept clarification using searches

The conceptual inventory so far has been of individual nodes and of the whole list. NVivo provides many tools for exploring the relations of nodes, and this may be a useful next strategy. The search operators offer a complete range of ways of playing with data. They allow you to pull apart material coded at a concept and tease out different meanings in it, seeking surprises and locating patterns. You may develop finer and subtler concepts, or alterntively see that there is a common thread running through the data, with contextually dependent variations in its expression.

By now you will be using both sets of nodes and node trees to keep ideas in order. Try playing them off against each other. Increasingly, you will find sets useful as temporary groupings for theory-exploring purposes. Using trees to clarify the logical relations of "catalogues" of ideas, you can play with sets to ask questions not about logic but about purpose and content of nodes. Which nodes really matter? Where is the conceptual system redundant? What can now be reduced, concentrated and developed?

Earlier, in Part 5, you used a Union search to see the degree of overlap between two nodes, and in Part 6 this was extended (using also Co-occurrence and Difference searches) to review the relationship between members of a set of nodes. Now that you have more documents coded, and it is increasingly clear which nodes are becoming important to your understanding of your topic, you might like to repeat or extend this exercise using either the same or different nodes.

"Playing" with searches

D.I.Y.

In the first instance, as you found before, use of Union, Co-occurrence and Difference searches will tell you whether a particular concept takes on different meanings, depending on whether another is present or absent in the text. Now you might try grouping together similar nodes (again using Union)—to create a "dump" of related ideas, and then "split" that node in new ways, to see if new dimensions are revealed within the text.

- To split the node, work with the Union node, or a modification of it, and pair that (using a Matrix Intersection) with the values of possibly relevant attributes, or with subcatgories in another tree (using either Matrix Intersection, or Matrix Co-occurrence).

- Browse the cells of the matrix, to see if the broad concept in the "dump node" is expressed differently in the different cells. If so, do these differences imply that there are quite different concepts within that node (perhaps some new ones to consider), or do they demonstrate that while there is conceptual coherence, the concept is simply taking on different dimensions in response to the presence of different conditions?

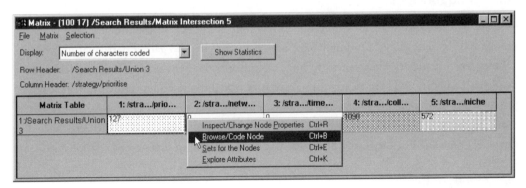

The result of your searching from this and the earlier exercise, then, might be

- combination of several nodes into one single node,

- retention of the original distinctions in the categories combined for the exercise,

- creation of new nodes reflecting newly revealed differences, or

- creation of a core category which has a number of contextually determined dimensions.

Use selected coding stripes to assist you in viewing and assessing your results.

You may find that you need to take some of the resulting nodes from your "splits" and explore their relationships with other (quite different) nodes in your project, as you continue your search for conceptual and theoretical integrity. This is the stage of a project where the concept of "playing" with the data takes on real meaning (but of course, in an entirely functional way!).

In the Project Journal in Researchers 4 you will find that I started to question the relationship between enjoyment, interest, passion, and intellectual stimulation, and to wonder if these could be best discriminated in terms of their intensity and/or in terms of their intellectual *vs* their emotional focus. Now <u>obsession</u> has been added, something which potentially brings together a set of categories reflecting emotional intensity (enjoyment, passion, addiction) with concepts reflecting behavioural intensity (e.g. commitment, persistence). Using the data in **Researchers 6** try grouping and regrouping these nodes (along with any others you think might be related) in the ways just described, to explore the best way of defining and locating them for this project. Then perhaps you will be able to answer the question raised in Researchers 4 and also perhaps to determine the potential value of obsession as a core category for (or essential element of) the experience of being a researcher.

Clustering concepts

Finally, a different strategy for exploring the relations of nodes is to examine the way categories "hang together". You may have been using the trees to gather particular nodes about generic categories like values, feelings or strategies. Perhaps there is some underlying construct which could help to explain or give structure to these nodes (rather like the way that factors do in quantitative research)? Of course, one way to do this is to read and reflect, seeking the more theoretical categories (perhaps "ideological constraints" rather than the generic "values"?) But the search processes may prove helpful in teasing out relationships.

Discovering clusters

D.I.Y.

You can use matrix searches to pair each of the subcategories with each other subcategory, much like creating a correlation matrix (to borrow again from statistical terminology). The numeric counts indicate whether there is a strong association between pairs of nodes, a clue to whether you might be able to reduce or pattern the subcategories used.

- Run a Boolean Matrix Intersection, with the Set or the Tree of nodes you are interested in entered identically in each of the "boxes" for the search.

- Scope the search to include only non-memo documents.

- Display document counts in the output matrix to provide a guide as to the patterns of relationships among the specific nodes. (The diagonal of the matrix showing the total number of documents in which any code appears.)

- Do you get a different pattern, or simply more finds, by using a Proximity (Matrix Co-occurrence) search? Ask for co-occurrences in the same paragraph or a specific section level (perhaps representing speaker turns, or questions, depending on how your documents were set up), and then, repeat the search asking for co-occurrences in the same document (Section level 0).

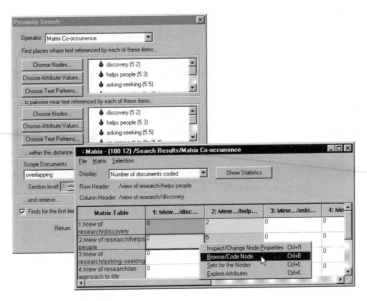

Now the qualitative task is to review the text in each of the cells (note: for one half of the matrix only, either above or below the diagonal), in order to check whether pairing was occurring because the documents referred to much the same thing (and so it got coded at both nodes), or whether it was because two quite different things were being contrasted (in which case, of course, "collapsing" those nodes would make no sense at all). If the numeric version of the clustering is shown (by the text version) to make sense in terms of these being pairs that really do go together, and you have a sufficient sample size, then you might want to export the matrix table to a statistics package, where it can be further analysed using either correspondence analysis or cluster analysis.

As a consequence of running such a procedure, you might then want to regroup your nodes, so that you can then look at and ask questions about the newly clustered concepts in relationship to other aspects of your project data.

Exploring and validating patterns

Qualitative researchers seek and explore patterns that are usually not clearcut. "Where does this attitude occur and can I understand why? How do these different ideas fit together in people's experience? Does a core category take different shapes under different conditions?" Pattern-seeking and validating techniques are part of the process of theorizing, of looking for the "missing links" in an emerging theory, of finding where it doesn't fit and testing the predictions that can be made from it.

Your question may be asking simply about the level of association between categories, for example, whether a particular view of research is associated with greater or lesser enthusiasm for research? You might then go on to seek further clarification or detail: does the personality of the researcher make a difference in this—or the availability of friends, family or colleagues who provide encouragement? The results of the first search can be coded-on and/or "fed in" to a further search in order to build an analysis. As you progress with your project and grow in sophistication in using the Search Tool, you will be able to make your searches increasingly targeted, detailed and specific—providing your node system and project structure allows it. Since the results of your searches are always coded at a node, they can be reflected upon, used iteratively in further searches, and/or stored as verification of conclusions.

What is going on here?

Qualitative pattern-seeking is often more like groping around than elegant hypothesis-testing. NVivo provides a number of tools for tentative pattern seeking. Many of the tools have been described already, in detail, including use of Union searches displayed with selected coding stripes (Parts 5 and 6), Co-occurrence of nodes (Part 6), Intersections of nodes with other nodes (Part 7) and Intersections of nodes and attributes (Part 8). Here we introduce new tools—assay and profiles—and searches that go a step (or two) further in order to ask and seek answers to more complex, and more theoretically productive, questions.

Assay the data

You may have noticed (and explored) the facility in NVivo to assay any part of your data for any specified feature. Assaying (a geological term) asks "What's here?" This may be a way of being surprised. As you explore the set of documents where a particular interpretation is expressed, you often wish to know more about them, for example: Are these interviews only from one age group? Do they all have coding at the node for a related issue? If not, which do?

Assay is accessed through the Scope panel in the Search Tool. You don't need to be doing a search (but if you are, the ability to assay the scope of that search can be very clarifying).

- Customize the scope to the documents and/or nodes do you want to examine. Choose to Assay Scope.

- Select an assay item. Below the list, you are shown the proportion of the scope documents and nodes in which that item occurs. (That may be the answer to your question—oops, there are no young interviewees in this scope!)

- To explore patterning of data, select a number of assay items—perhaps all nodes in a tree, or a set, maybe along with some attribute values—and click Make Assay Profile. A table is displayed, showing occurrences of those items for the scope documents or nodes.

- Now change the scope. Does that impact on the presence or absence of your selected nodes? Does the pattern change? Used in this way, assay will provide pointers to where you might fruitfully search. From the searches, you can review the text to validate and determine the meaning of any emergent patterns.

View coding profiles

A profile of coding, either for a set of documents or for a set of nodes, offers a summary of where nodes are being used across documents. This can be a fertile ground for early theorizing. It provides a tabular overview of how nodes are used and allows you to compare and contrast the patterns of coding. Do the patterns match with your overall impressions? Is there anything you have missed? Are there nodes you have developed since your first document(s) or that you were not emphasizing at that stage? Are there common elements across the documents, suggesting common experiences or processes. Do you need to check whether you have used labels in a consistent way?

- From the Nodes menu at the top of the Project Pad, select Profile Coding for All Nodes. Ask for the Number of Passages.

- A new dialogue will ask for the Set of Documents to profile coding from. If you want to profile coding of all your documents, leave this as it is. (All Documents is a set made for you as the documents are created.) If you want to view the coding patterns for a particular document set (for example, for Interviews only), click on Choose, then double click on Sets, select the set, and click OK.

- From the resulting profile, review which nodes were used for which documents. Note those that warrant further thought or investigation.

This is also a neat way of comparing how team members are coding, or checking your changing use of nodes over time. Code two copies of the same document, make a set of them, and profile the coding from just those two.

Seeking associations

Associations between one feature and another in the data can be explored through searches. How do you find which is the best choice of search operator to use?

At this advanced stage, a review of the way searches work will help you in designing search strategies. The logical Boolean search operators are appropriate only for some questions. Are you seeking the association of the values of an document's attribute (age, for example) with coding at nodes? This is a clear case for Boolean searches, and they will always find patterns if there are any to find. Since the attribute applies to the whole document, any text coded at the node will intersect with that attribute. But Boolean searches may be less useful when asking for associations between the ideas represented by nodes, since these are unlikely to occur in the text in neat intersections. (How do people's attitudes to research seem to fit with approaches to professional career advancement?) The Proximity searches will be more useful here, as they retrieve all the relevant material in the particular document or section—even where an intersection does not occur.

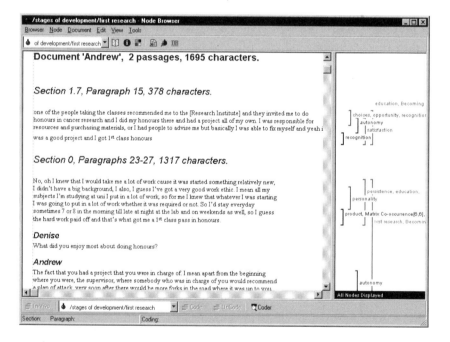

Is viewing research in discovery terms associated with enthusiasm for research? In terms of my nodes the latter might have been expressed simply as <u>identification</u> as a researcher (as distinct from a teacher or business person), as <u>enjoyment</u> of research, or at another level again, as <u>obsession</u> with research. It is unlikely that the node for discovery and a node related to enthusiasm would occur on exactly the same text, or even nearby within a document, so Intersect or Overlap may get nothing. But there may be a looser association—if people talk this way, what do they say about that? Such a question will be best answered using a Proximity Co-occurrence search in which the node for <u>view of research as discovery</u> and for <u>enthusiasm</u> will be found if they exist in the same document (Section level 0), with the search scoped to include only those documents which represent a single viewpoint (excluding focus group documents, for example).

But then, does this association exist only for those who are more (or less) experienced researchers? Or for those who have a particular educational background? Change the scope for the search (e.g. from interviews in general to interviews with beginner and early career researchers and then interviews with more experienced researchers) to see if the character of the association changes. Or undertake a further proximity search in which the results of the first search (association between discovery and enthusiasm) are further associated with educational background (again, using Co-occurrence in same document). View coding stripes in the Node Browser whilst reading the resulting text, to get ideas about what else is going on here.

So discovery is associated with enthusiasm for certain groups only in certain documents. But perhaps those who view research in terms of application or as a craft are just as enthusiastic (or even more so) about doing research? Change the node specification to view the changes (or run as a matrix).

Under what conditions…?

Much qualitative research seeks not direct associations between categories or features but the fit between a phenomenon and a context. Grounded theorists, for example, may work to build a conditional matrix displaying under what conditions certain events (or issues or values) are associated with certain consequences (or outcomes). If the context (i.e. the circumstances surrounding the event) changes, does that mean the outcome changes? Does the category take on different expressions under different circumstances, while still retaining its conceptual integrity?

At this stage of theory-work, the Node Browser is often the crucial tool, since it shows you all the different material at this category, but only a click away from the original documents. After working with the coded material to develop the category being explored, you may find the search techniques outlined above (looking at single associations, then scoping to different groups or nodes, adding in a further variable).

If all three elements in the question—events (or issues or values), circumstances and outcomes—have been coded throughout the documents, searches can be used to locate and differentiate the text. Your task, again, is to read and interpret the text, to find answers to the question of association.

The understanding of conditions is a good example of how qualitative questions may evade search processes. The researcher often does not see context as important—taking it for granted, just as does the participant, and so coding has not recorded it. Only as the analysis proceeds is the relevance of this context discovered. (In Part 7 we noted the value of the tree structure in ensuring comprehensive coding of elements like contextual circumstances.)

Exploring patterns with searches

For exploring and checking an emerging idea, use matrix searches to give you a different sort of access to the text. These searches are unlikely to be the end of your theoretical road, but may point to where more detailed investigation needs to take place.

- Select a category whose conditions you are trying to understand. Browse the node and read, writing a memo on patterns you think you are finding.

- For an initial review of the patterns of relationships, build a matrix, for example, of events by circumstances. Which kind of events are most likely to occur under which circumstances? View the matrix first in crude coding density terms—the number of times different events occurred in different circumstances. What does this tell you? If there is inadequate data in each cell; seek an explanation. (There isn't any story to tell? You didn't code these elements thoroughly? You need to seek more evidence?)

- Now examine whether circumstance changes an issue, and how a particular issue (or event) is spoken of under different circumstances. Browse the nodes for the critical cells, writing in the relevant memos about what you find.

- What do these associations then mean in terms of outcomes (or consequences)? You might take case studies from the extremes of the outcomes, and return to all the material about each case to account fully for the ways that context is related to the phenomenon studied. Seek more detailed understanding of issues or aspects that matter particularly in the case, then look more broadly at these, across cases.

- Armed by this growing understanding, return to searching, with a matrix co-occurrence of the event/s by the outcome/s. Examine what happens (to both numbers and text) if the scope is changed to include only documents where particular circumstances are indicated (filter the document set by coding or attributes).

 As you flick the scope and rerun the search, remember to record in memos what you are seeing, and to code the memos as you write! The facility to shift scope and look again allows rapid-snapshot viewing of data, but also requires careful recording!

Investigating exceptions

It is not enough to know that a pattern exists, one also needs to know when it doesn't exist. Does its non-existence in some cases mean that the pattern or "theory" in fact doesn't hold, or is there an explanation—an additional refinement to be made to the theory?

Perhaps you need to include additional variables in the analysis, perhaps all that is needed is to carefully read through a deviant case to understand why it doesn't fit, and whether that invalidates the earlier conclusion or not, or perhaps new data will need to be sought, to fill out and test that explanation for the deviance.

Deviant cases are precious in providing important clues that will help to refine a theory. Always check to see if there is someone or something that doesn't fit the pattern, then investigate that case to figure why that is so. Use coding stripes to surprise you. Which text coded at this node *isn't* coded at this other? Use the Search Tool to locate not only the data that fits, but also the exceptions. In which documents does this association not hold? Which cases don't contain coding from any of this set of nodes? (The relevant search is probably the Boolean Difference, or it may be a Node Lookup, scoped to documents *not coded* at a particular node.)

Fine reading, detailed understanding

The tools described so far rely either on coding of documents or on the content of text retrieved. Your project may have developed less by coding of content than by use of the other tools for fine examination and interpretation of text, exploration of discourse, or analysis of the processes and structure of narrative. Where the investigation is of the *form* of the data, the analytical goals will be different and the processes of getting there require other steps.

The researcher studying the form of expression will have exploited rich text editing, annotation, text search, and the ability to hyperlink, via DataBites, to external files. If the text has been finely annotated and linked to soundbites and photographs, how is this now much more complex data to be brought together as an overview is sought?

If you have relied so far on content coding, moving to fine detailed examination of text may assist you to achieve a different level of analysis. If your methods do not direct you in this way, you may find reading in discourse analysis or grounded theory informs. Both will direct you (for different purposes) to greater reliance on memos and annotations. Trace changes in discourse or emotion as events are retold, or during the course of an interview. To do this, annotate the text (in DataBites) or record peaks and troughs and changes in document memos (and code these so that all this information can be "pulled together" for further analysis). Use color to draw your attention to powerful expressions or metaphors in the text. You may also find it useful to code for the style of language used, in addition to and separately from the content.

I've been re-reading what's coded at <u>identification</u> and was fascinated by the varied imagery and different meanings of identification. The thoughts were triggered by a passage in Frank's and Andrew's interviews. Frank talks of having "the research culture in me", and later of getting it "into you"—the imagery of penetration of self intrigues—while Andrew writes that he now recognizes he has "a passion for research [which] cannot be extinguished"—suggestive of an uncontrollable fire (or what, colloquially, would be referrred to as "fire in the belly") having been lit. These very powerful images contrast strongly with those of others who spoke much less emotively, for example, of research "always being there", or of seeing research as being secondary to some other direction.

D. I. Y.

New uses for text search

Does the language being used tell us about experience or expectation? What metaphors are there, and what do they signify? In earlier Parts, text search was introduced as a mechanical way of finding occurrences of a word or phrase and coding them. Rethink it now, as a way of accessing the range of meanings of a word, and understanding them in context.

- Run a text search, scoped to the relevant documents, e.g. interviews, for a term that intrigues or puzzles you. (Customize results and spread to include paragraphs.) Browse the results node and note the range of meanings, examine how that word is being used in different contexts and write about its uses.

- Run a text search for instances of a word or string of words (remember the option for alternation) and scope the search to the node or nodes identifying an issue or topic within which these words seem significant. For example, when the worker is talking about the union, does he use "we-us" or "they-them" to refer to what the union does?

Using reports as data

If you make use of DataBites and DataLinks, you can exploit the ability to report on documents or nodes with these links showing as endnotes.

- In the Document Explorer, select a document in which your fine analysis of the text has resulted in embedded annotations or links to external files or NVivo documents or nodes. From the Node menu, select Make Coding Report, and check Show DataLink details as endnotes. Click OK. View coding stripes to see which other nodes are associated with the annotated passages.

- The resulting report is a rich text file with numbers where your links were placed. At the end are numbered endnotes giving all text of your annotations and the details of other links to external files or NVivo documents or nodes.

- Save the document as RTF and it can be opened in rich text in your word processor—ready as a potential case study for the chapter or paper you are writing on this fine-detailed analysis.

- Now in the Node Explorer, select a node at which you have coded, annotated or linked data. Those links are live in the node. From the Node menu, select Make Coding Report, and check Show DataLink details as endnotes. Click OK.

These reports allow you to see and seek commonalities in the annotations. Your detailed commentary is now available for synthesis and development.

Insight, surprise and arrival

Being surprised is central to the qualitative task. We argued early in this book that all qualitative research is seeking new understanding from the data. To that end, data are kept rich, and access retained to context, as the researcher strives to find a new account of what is going on, a new synthesis of viewpoints, a new explanation of a problem or understanding of a process. Until the end of a project, the researcher is always seeking the unexpected, finding rewards in the unpredicted. Such moments are of great value in challenging assumptions, reviewing data, revising explanations and often in stimulating the bringing-together of a theory or an account of the situation studied.

Creating surprises

To *create* surprise is something of a contradiction. At this stage as a project consolidates, it also becomes more important. As your data processing becomes more confident, your node system more elegant, your coding more competent, there is a serious risk of routinisation. We have earlier warned against coding that becomes ritualistic. Here we raise an issue that concerns all qualitative methods: how to keep seeing your data anew?

Through this book we have described many ways to use NVivo to generate discovery, through editing and annotating text, "playing" with categories and developing concepts, seeking and validating patterns, asking questions of your data and working with the answers.

Using models for surprise

D.I.Y.

By now the models you sketched earlier may begin to look simplistic. Worse, they may seem to spatter ideas, rather than bring them together. If this is happening, revisit the model's interplaying tools for grouping and layering. Groups are constructed in a similar way to layers, but are independent of them. These then give two different, crosscutting, ways of expressing how ideas go together. Try flicking between layers, selecting different groups. You may find that you see, for example, the ways that a group of cases repeatedly occur in different stages of a process.

- Select the items you wish to include in a group (probably while in the All layer): you can multiple select by using Ctrl-click.

- With your mouse cursor (arrow) located over one of the selected items, click on your right mouse button to access the context menu.

- Choose Group then New from the context menu. Provide a name for the new group. Repeat for a second group.

To add new items to an existing group:

- Select (highlight) the item.
- From the context menu, choose Group.
- Select the Group you want to add the item to.

To view groups:

- From the View menu, select Groups Palette (or click the [icon] icon in the toolbar).
- In the Show Groups dialogue, check against the groups you wish to have displayed. Members of these will become highlighted in the model being viewed.

Use models both to assist in clarifying what you are seeing, and eventually to synthesise it so others can see it too. Attempting to present your conclusions in the form of a model at once reveals where links are missing, and "forces" you toward possible solutions, or pathways. Aim to simplify your model: often you will develop a very complex picture of the story you want to tell from your data, taking into account every detail you have explored. But then, a good theory has a degree of simplicity: can you identify the core of your ideas and present those in a coherent way that remains true to your data?

Different data

Built into many qualitative methods is the assumption that during a project the researcher will re-sample, using techniques of data-driven "theoretical sampling". This means seeking new data when the growing theory directs that a new area be investigated.

Given the tools for data management in NVivo, the seeking of new data, from a different source or of a different type, need not be alarming. Attributes and sets can clearly identify the different data documents, and you have the ability to play one source or sort of data off against the other. This process may be another source of new insight. In the Researchers Project, for example, the focus group with students offered quite new meanings of research and interpretations of research motivation from those in the interviews with established researchers.

Searching for surprises

In our detailed discussions of searches for pattern seeking and validating, we omitted to mention that often their most valuable role may be to surprise. Using the Assay and Scope tools alongside the search procedures, you will regularly be presented with results that are unexpected. The association *disappears* when the scope excludes those early interviews? Why would that be? The friction of such results too often merely annoys—unless you have methods for using and retaining surprises.

Using (rather than losing) surprises

A common experience in this sort of research is that the little occurrences of surprises are overtaken by the momentum of data processing. Odd ideas are forgotten, the results of unintended inquiries deleted, startling idiosyncratic discoveries overlooked in favor of consistent patterns. When a recurrence occurs ("Where have I heard that expression before?") it may be too late to develop the link with the earlier surprise that was let go. But the advice to hold onto all surprises for ever would be clearly impractical, and the majority of surprises certainly do not promise a straight line to the research goal. Some odd ideas just are odd! So how can you manage surprise generation and retention in the next stage of getting there?

Storing surprises

Anselm Strauss remarked to one of us, "If it matters, it will come up again." This is a controversial statement, since it implies that unique occurrences don't matter. But here we are concerned with its other implication, that you need to know when something comes up *again*. There are many ways to use the tools of NVivo to store surprises.

- Make a node for <u>Surprising</u>! In its properties box give it a way-out number and it will turn up at the end of any List of all nodes. Code at it oddities and memos about them, and whenever you are stuck in your interpretation of a category or document you can ask to see everything in it that is also coded at the <u>Surprising</u> node.

- As you order categories into trees, make a set for all the nodes that indicate "odd" or surprising categories. As odd ideas or search results occur, include these nodes in the Surprises set. It will soon hold an amazing array of items, many of which should never see public display! But by storing them there you keep them safe, just in case that comes up again. If the idea recurs, it is likely to find a place in the main node system.

Memos as surprise holders

In many ways the strategies you adopt for qualitative analysis will be similar to those used for any analysis, with the most critical element always being the ability to ask questions of the data: "I wonder if...?" By now your memos are likely to be full of questions (clearly visible where color has been used to identify them), so reviewing the questions asked throughout your memos is a good starting place.

- NVivo makes a set of all memos. In the Document Set Editor assess the body of memos, and to ask questions of your memos. It may be a surprise just to find you wrote a memo on a topic that has reasserted itself as critical!

- NVivo memos are full status documents: are you coding them, so that you can query their contents? (For this core category: how often is there coding from memos at the node?) Filter the memos in the Document Set Editor, to find which have coding at important nodes. Profile the coding of all memos.

When is an "Aha" a final chapter?

All qualitative research methods involve arrival at an explanation or account that "makes sense" of what has been studied. Once more, we advise return to the methods literature for techniques and examples. Much of the literature suggests that "making sense", or arrival, is a mystical process, beyond technical discussion, and so mystique may prevent your finding a pathway for your own analysis.

Making sense, or arriving at a conclusion, can mean many things to different researchers. Sometimes they are referring to discovery of a new way of viewing variation across the data that is quite different from those that were brought to the data or previously seen. The "aha" then comes from surprise, the significant missing link suddenly seen. But getting there is much more than getting a new idea. The process of arrival at an analytical end involves completeness and adequacy of explanation, not just surprise. From now on, your use of the tools in NVivo will be informed by the goal that things are to come together, relationships are to be uncovered or links explained, before the project's purposes are satisfied.

How will you know when an account is good enough? In the preceding sections we have outlined tools for testing and profiling, interrogating and interpreting patterns and themes in the data. We conclude with the tools for displaying, reviewing and reporting.

Showing and Telling

A crucial part of the arrival process is reporting—not merely at the end, to fulfil the requirements of the degree or grants body, but much more importantly to bring things together in your own mind. Finding an answer will always be assisted by writing as you go, by recording what you learn from each analysis, even if that was "nothing". The act of trying to write it down and make sense of it all will prompt further questions and searching of data, until the focus is clear and you can see that you have a coherent story to tell. NVivo offers tools for attractive and sophisticated ways of telling the story, by visual display or printed report. Draft, redraft and then rewrite any account of the data, either in NVivo's editor or in a word processor. The process of writing is always clarifying (even if it gloomily shows that you still know too little to write it up!)

Memos are also data

Memos in NVivo and papers out of it may be the most useful pathway to a satisfying account. The following techniques and tactics may enrich your writing and enhance its contribution to analysis.

- Always treat memos as full status documents, and code and search them, so your ideas are data, appearing and/or contrasted with the data from other sources.
- Date memo edits to keep a project history in the memos of the central nodes.
- Use the ability to copy and paste text from a document or node into any other document (e.g. a memo) or to link Extract Nodes to build up full accounts of the data to support your interpretation. Note that the coding is preserved too, so that when you are discussing a passage from a document, you can view its coding as you write your interpretation.

Ways to display

Display and discussion to members of a team, a peer audience or supervisors may be the most immediate way of assisting the coming-together of your project. For this purpose, the modeler provides an unusual medium, a change from standard presentation formats. The display of your presentation can directly call the data you are discussing.

Construct a model that shows how you are interpreting your data currently. Now to make it a presentation tool:

- Use layers to show how your understanding has grown
- Add documents, including memos, and nodes to indicate the crucial data at different parts of the model.

- Within the documents in the model, use Extract Nodes to bring up the pertinent quotations and DataBites to run a sound or video clip.

- Add models of particular issues, situations etc. These nested models are live, like the documents and nodes, and can be opened at a mouseclick (or link to the previous model via a DataBite in the document that is live in the present model).

Now run it! The model contains the live links to all the aspects of the project you may wish to discuss. Click on them to display and illustrate as you give your account of the data.

Viewing a project

As your project develops, you may wish to have a colleague, client or supervisor view and explore it—without risking your work! Give them the NVivo Viewer, a free version of the software which (like the version in the back of this book) will allow any NVivo process except saving. Any of the tools explored in this Part can be used by the person viewing a project as they review your categories and coding, read your memos, try new searches and evaluate your work. Prepare a document summarizing the issues to be explored and containing hyperlinks to the relevant data, nodes or memos: the person viewing can jump from these links to explore the desired aspects of the project. Alternatively, give access to the viewer via a model such as described.

Making reports

Text, numeric and diagrammatic reports can all be generated from NVivo to use in putting together your final report. As you prepare reports, ensure that you are using the advantages of rich text and the many modes of tabular display available.

Draw on your memos and Project Journal when recording your conclusions. Text can be copied directly from these into a final report using the usual Cut and Paste operations. As a first step in bringing it all together, try writing the story of your research or presenting your theory by building your argument for your conclusions from the data, but without relying on direct quotations from the data to say it for you. Having detailed the basis of each of your claims to analysis, you can then incorporate illustrative text from documents or nodes. This can be copied and pasted directly from the Browsers or alternatively, from a rich text report of a document or a coding report of a node.

If you are saving a text report so that it can be opened in your word processor, be sure to save it in .rtf format rather than .txt, so that you preserve any formatting in that text.

You can incorporate tabular data generated from profiles or assaying into your report. You might begin by using assaying or an attribute table to describe your sample, so that your audience can properly assess the significance and generality of your conclusions. Further assay tables in the body of the report may most succinctly show the patterning you want to demonstrate. Avoid generalities ("most"; "some") when you can be specific (15 of the 17 reported...; 35% of these instances...). You might export your assay or profile first to a spreadsheet, so that it can be turned into a graph to illustrate a point you want to make, for example, about the changes in frequency of reference to something, use of a term, or differences across groups. Options for printing or exporting tables are found under the File menu within the Assay or Profile or Attribute Explorer windows.

If you are exporting tables to a word processor, change the tab settings, or the font style (to a monospace font) or use a Text to Table option to ensure that the tables "line up" neatly.

A model can be exported for inclusion in a report by first saving it to the clipboard (in NVivo), then pasting it directly, as a picture, into a word processor document.

Most importantly, when writing a report, paper, chapter or thesis, draw on the notes you have made throughout the project to show how you have arrived at your conclusions. Qualitative researchers differ markedly in their thinking about what makes for rigor in qualitative research, but primarily it will boil down to how convincing you can be in showing how you arrived at the conclusions you reached.

What next to learn about NVivo?

Of course, there are many tools and many strategies not explored in this book. You will constantly discover more functions and techniques in NVivo from your reading of the books accompanying the software, from listening to other researchers discuss their strategies, from helping others with their data puzzles, from clicking around and experimenting, from reading the Help files (remember to press F1 in any window to get context-sensitive Help).

Please don't wait till you have learned everything in the software before you get on with your research. Your project is underway, and the tools you have now used will support a wide range of research strategies. If you have followed the steps through this book, your knowledge of the software is considerable.

The project isn't finished or the final report written. This may not happen for some time, but one way of telling the software tools are being used skilfully and even that the end is in sight is that at this stage, the questions are different, and the ways of asking them are increasingly accessible.

This book concludes with an Appendix of advice for preparing data—and our best wishes for your research.

Appendix: Preparing Data

A minimum of preparation is needed for documents to be imported into NVivo. Documents are prepared and saved in rich text format using Word or Wordpad so that formatting can be preserved, or in plain text using any word processor. Data files containing document information (attributes) can be prepared in any table-based software (such as Excel), and saved as tab-delimited text.

Preparing a text document for import into NVivo

A document needs a name. It can also have:

a)   a description;

b)   subheadings which define sections in your document; and

c)   text.

There are advantages to be gained, however, when thought is given to the way in which the document is structured. Structure is achieved primarily through the use of heading styles, which can define up to nine levels of subsection in the document. If your document is in plain text, NVivo will recognise mark-up symbols to identify the document name and description, and to give style to your document.

Making notes or transcriptions

When you're making notes from or transcribing your interview, focus group or field observations, remember to make use of the font styles in your word processor (e.g. **bold**, *italics*) to help convey the subtleties of what is happening—emphasis, uncertainty, excitement, an aside. You may need to note events, e.g. (tape off), (telephone rings) or spell out some of the nonverbal things that happen, such as (pause), (long pause), (laughter). As you're listening to a tape and taking notes or transcribing, you may come to some point in the conversation that is particularly interesting or potent, or an amusing exchange. Put a reminder to yourself into the notes/transcript as to where that interesting bit is (e.g. count 340). You may wish to make a DataBite to link directly from your document to the external file with the tape extract.

Rich text documents

Text in an NVivo document can incorporate most of the familiar richness of appearance that word processors provide, such as changes in font type, size and style, colour, spacing, justification, indents and tabs. Use this to help you shape your data, express emphasis in field notes, or clarify how your respondents were expressing themselves. The text will retain its formatting when imported into NVivo. Note that NVivo cannot import documents containing embedded objects such as tables and pictures. Further detail about what will prevent import, or will be dropped from the imported document, is available in the Reference Manual, Appendix A.

Use headings throughout the text to clarify its presentation and to create sections within the document. For example, in a structured questionnaire or interview, headings would be used to indicate the content of the text that follows; in a less structured interview, speaker names might be set out as headings, so that turns in conversation become sections in the document. With NVivo, up to nine levels of heading are available, so that it is possible to have sections within sections, thus, for example, it is possible to have topic headings, and then within those, speaker headings. Styles are used to identify the headings: NVivo will not see text as a heading just because it is bold or in a different font. When Styles have been used, any retrieval (including those from a text search) can easily be spread to include the section from which the retrieval came, giving rapid access to the topic being discussed at the time, or to who said that, or the date or site or circumstances of the events being described. Similarly, in a structured questionnaire, labelling a question using a heading style allows searching with spreading to automatically find and code all the responses.

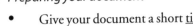

Preparing your document

D.I.Y.
- Give your document a short <u>title</u> (optional: you can alternatively tell NVivo to read the file name as its title).

- Take a new paragraph. Add a <u>description</u> to the top of your document, to remind you how you made it. You might record when, where and perhaps why the data was collected, by whom, and any special notes about the circumstances. Note that the description has to be set up within a single paragraph. It can be accessed at any time through Properties, or in reports.

- Then it's a matter of typing up your <u>text</u>, inserting <u>headings</u> as appropriate. You will need to take a new line after each heading. If you are working in your word processor, the text should automatically revert to "normal style" when you do so. Use headings at different levels for different purposes (think strategically about this!).

- Save your document in Rich Text Format (.rtf) using Microsoft Word. Rich text format can be selected from the Save file as type: slot at the base of the Save As dialogue. You do not need to save your document in any particular folder in order to access it from NVivo, although the Source Documents folder in the All Users folder for your project has been provided as a convenient place to store original documents.

NVivo will create the document name and description for your imported document in either of two ways:

1) the source file name will become the name of the document, and the first paragraph will be the description;

2) the first paragraph will be read as the document name, and the second as the description.

You can change these later, or add to the description, in the Document Properties box.

Don't worry if you haven't got the document exactly right, because it is possible to edit it after you have imported it, just as you can in a word processor.

Tip If your computer has a standard screen (800 x 600 pixels) then, before the final save for your documents select all the text and drag the right indent marker in to around the 12 cm mark. That way, when you are viewing your document in NVivo with the Coder open as well, your text will not be obscured.

Using search and replace to make headings

To get your speaker names (or topics or whatever you are using as subheadings) into Heading Level 2 style (or whatever level you want) without having to do each entry individually, or even each speaker individually, use a : (colon) after each when you are typing up (make it something different for each level of heading). Then use search and replace in MS Word to change the style of the colon from Normal to, say, Heading 2. It will change the whole paragraph (in this case, the name as well as the colon).

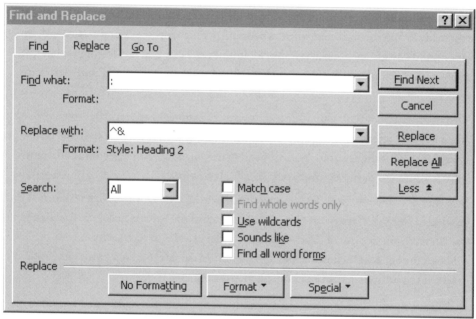

To search for text and replace with a Style:

- Place your cursor at the beginning of the text which includes headings you wish to change to a Heading Style.

- Open the Replace box (Edit menu) and click on **More**. In the Find what: slot, type in the character you have used to identify your headings (such as :). In the Replace with: slot, type the same character or add the Find What Text item from the **Special** list (assuming you still want it as part of your text, otherwise, leave blank).

- Make sure your cursor is in the Replace with: slot (it usually jumps back to the first one) and click on Format at the bottom of the Find and Replace box. Choose Style and then select the heading style you want for that text. You will notice that under Replace with: there is now a note indicating Format: Style: Heading 2.

- Finally, click on Replace All, and Word will turn all your marked text into styled headings. Note that if you want to use Replace without Styles in the same work session, you will have to choose No Formatting to remove the Style option.

Tip For interview data: Ensure you are consistent in using the same level of heading for speakers across your documents, as this will affect retrievals when carrying out Proximity searches. Avoid using Heading 1 for speakers, in case you decide to add in topic headings as you work through an interview. Some researchers have found it useful to use Heading 2 for the interviewer, and Heading 3 for the respondent. When they are retrieving context for coded segments, then, they can see firstly all that the respondent said (View enclosing section) and then what the interviewer said that prompted the response (View enclosing section, again) without needing to browse the whole document.

Preparing open-ended survey responses

It is advisable to use a Word template (.dot file) for preparing survey documents (an NVivo.dot file is provided on the software CD) where questions have been asked in a fixed order. With a template, responses given to open ended questions can be typed under standardized headings for each question, both saving time for the typist, and ensuring that all headings are exactly the same.

The temptation for some researchers is to type up all the answers to a single question as a single document, but doing so places great limitations on the capacity for analysis. There should be a separate document prepared for each respondent. This is important for being able to import attribute data, to allow document (and therefore respondent) counts of coding as an adjunct to the statistical analysis of the data, and to enable comparison of responses, on an individual basis, across questions (How did those who raised this issue in response to that question respond to the question about the other?).

If the automatic Section Coder is to be used (advisable where you have many questions), then use Heading 1 style for your main questions, and then Heading 2 for subquestions, and so on. NVivo will then create a node structure which will parallel the outline structure of the document. If you plan to use text search instead (with spread to sections) to code your responses (advisable where you have many respondents and few questions), ensure that the headings used start with distinctive characters or contain unique keywords (i.e. ones which are not included anywhere in the general text).

Preparing a plain text document—with *style*

Email messages can provide a rich source of data for particular research projects (cf. the Bush Schooling tutorial provided with your NVivo disk), but these are typically in plain text format. Other data sources too may come as plain text, particularly if they have had to be transferred from other word processors (such as older versions of WordPerfect). Or you may have precious data in a NUD*IST project which you want to incorporate into your new NVivo project. That data, too, will have been saved in plain text format, or as text with line breaks. (If you want to convert your NUD*IST project to NVivo as a whole, complete with coding and memos, that is a different issue—a full description of how to do that is provided in the Reference Manual, chapter 12.)

One could go through each document manually, either in a word processor, or in NVivo, inserting headings and other features. Sometimes all that is needed, or appropriate, is to provide a title and description for the document. Where there is some repetition, however, the more efficient alternative may be to use "search and replace" in your word processor to tidy your document, and to insert mark up indicators to tell NVivo which text you want as title, description, or section headings.

NVivo recognises the following mark up symbols:

{t} Title

{d} Description

{h1} Heading Level 1

{h2} Heading Level 2

etc. to {h9}.

These should be placed at the beginning of the first line for the relevant paragraph (leave a space after the closing bracket). Text in that paragraph will then be given the style indicated by the symbol when the document is imported into NVivo. Note that NVivo will recognise these mark up symbols only in plain text documents.

Often search and replace can be used to speed the process of inserting the mark up symbols.

Preparing data for attribute import

Importing attribute information from a table provides a rapid alternative to defining and entering attributes one at a time. Attributes for either documents or nodes can be entered in much the same way. Typically this data is entered in a spreadsheet such as Excel, but it may also be imported from a statistical or any other database. If it is being imported from SPSS or an alternative database that will export variables in numeric format only, then it may be necessary to transfer the data via a spreadsheet, as described below.

D.I.Y.

Using Excel to prepare document attribute data

- Open a new file in Excel.

- At the top of the first column, type the word "Document".

- Going across (use tab to move to the next cell), enter the names of your attributes at the tops of columns, one to each column. If any of these have already been created within NVivo, then be sure to spell it the same way, with the same capitalization.

- In the first column (headed "Document") list the names for each of your documents, exactly as they are entered in NVivo. They do not have to be in any special order.

- Create a matrix of values by typing into each cell the value that applies to the document and attribute that intersect there.

- Save your file in Excel format (you will need to return to this format if you wish to update the file for additional documents later).

- Now choose Save As from the File menu. At the bottom of the Save As dialogue, where it says Save as type: choose Text (tab delimited) (*.txt).

- Close your file (and Excel). (Be careful not to agree to reconvert your file to Excel format as you do this.)

Using Word to prepare data

- Set a series of Left Tabs across the page of a new document at, say, 5 cm spacing. You will need one tab mark for each attribute you wish to assign to your documents. (You may need to turn your page to landscape view, to fit in as many as you want.)

- Type the word Document at the beginning of the first line, then tab to the next position.

- Type the first attribute name in the next position, then tab across, type the next, and so on. Make sure that *none* of your entries takes you into the next tab space (if it must, then select your whole document, and move the tab mark across for that column).

- On the next line, type the first document name, exactly as it is in NVivo. Tab across and enter the value for that document for the first attribute. Tab across and enter the next value for the next attribute, and so on. Tab to leave an empty "cell" for any missing values.

- Repeat these steps for each document.

- Save your file as a Text Only document. Close the document.

Preparing a Node Attribute table

- Open a new file in Excel (or other table based software).

- At the top of the first column, type the word "Node".

- Going across (use tab to move to the next cell), enter the names of your attributes at the tops of columns, one to each column. If any of these have already been created within NVivo, then be sure to spell it the same way, with the same capitalization.

- In the first column (headed "Node".) list the names for each of your nodes e.g. case nodes. Full node titles must be used, or use node addresses (enclosed in parentheses) for Tree Nodes. The format for typing a case node title is .casetype:casenode or perhaps .casetype.casetype:casenode depending on the structure of the case types. Thus, for Fred who is a group participant, the node title would be .Group1:Fred (Capitalization must match that used in the Node Explorer.)

- Create a matrix of values by typing into each cell the value that applies to the case node and the attribute that intersect there, e.g. male for Fred. Make sure you enter only one value per cell.

- Save your file in Excel format (you will need to return to this format if you wish to update the file for additional documents later).

- Now choose Save As from the File menu. At the bottom of the Save As dialogue, where it says Save as type: choose Text (tab delimited) (*.txt).

- Close your file (and Excel). (Be careful not to agree to reconvert your file to Excel format as you do this.)

Retaining value labels rather than numbers from an SPSS file

When you save your SPSS data as a text file, values will be saved in their numeric form, even if value labels are showing on the SPSS data screen. This means that when you import the table into NVivo the string attributes will (inconveniently) have numeric rather than text labels. This can be overcome by using Excel (or another spreadsheet) as an intermediate step.

- First, save your (cut down) SPSS data as an Excel file, requesting that the first row be read as variable names.

- Open the file in Excel. (Apart from the variable names in the first row, data will be shown in numeric form.)

- Return to SPSS. Make sure value labels are showing (check Value Labels in the View menu).

- Select the whole SPSS database, and Copy it. (Note: only the values are copied, not the variable names.)

- Return to Excel. Select cell **A2** (so as to leave variable names intact), and Paste. (If you are using an older version of Excel, highlight all the numeric data to give you the correct area, then Paste.) You will now have a spreadsheet with variable names and value labels rather than numeric codes.

- Save as a tab-delimited text file, ready for import to NVivo.

Index